Canícula

NORMA ELIA CANTÚ

CANÍCULA

Snapshots of a Girlhood
en la Frontera

UNIVERSITY OF NEW MEXICO PRESS
Albuquerque

18 17 16 15 14   9 10 11 12 13

Paperbound ISBN-13: 978-0-8263-1828-2

Library of Congress Cataloging-in Publication Data

Cantú, Norma Elia, 1947–
Canícula : snapshots of a girlhood en la frontera / Norma Elia
Cantú.—1st ed.   p. cm.
ISBN 0-8263-1592-5 : ISBN 0-8263-1828-2 (pbk.)
1. Mexican American families—Texas—Fiction. 2. Family—
Texas—Fiction. 3. Girls—Texas—Fiction. I. Title.
PS3553.A555C36   1995 813'.54—dc20   94-27153 CIP

Designed by Linda Mae Tratechaud
Title page photograph by Norman Johnson

Earlier versions of sections of this manuscript were previously published
in *The Texas Journal*, Spring, 1992; *Prarie Schooner*, Winter 1994;
and in the exhibition catalogue for *Dar a Luz*, Anne Wallace, 1992.

For my family on both sides of the border

Brinca la tablita,
Yo ya la brinqué,
Bríncala de vuelta,
Yo ya me cansé.

Children's game

All photographs are *memento mori*.

Susan Sontag

The U.S.–Mexican border es una herida abierta
where the Third World grates against the first and bleeds.

Gloria Anzaldúa

ᴗ Contents ᴗ

↣ Acknowledgments ↢

I acknowledge all who helped make this project happen. I thank Eloísa Ramón García, Florentino Cantú Vargas and Virginia Ramón Cantú for the stories and the photographs. I also thank Elsa Ruiz, Sandra Cisneros, Tey Diana Rebolledo, Ellie Hernández, Anne Wallace, Andrea Otañez and Barbara Guth for their support and encouragement. My gratitude to Elvia Niebla for the use of her laptop and to Ana Castillo for the use of her Santuario. To everyone who was there for me, inspired, listened, shared, and in innumerable ways touched my life I offer my sincere gratitude. Finally, and always, I acknowledge the Creator, the Universe in all its manifestations that guides my every step. ¡Gracias!

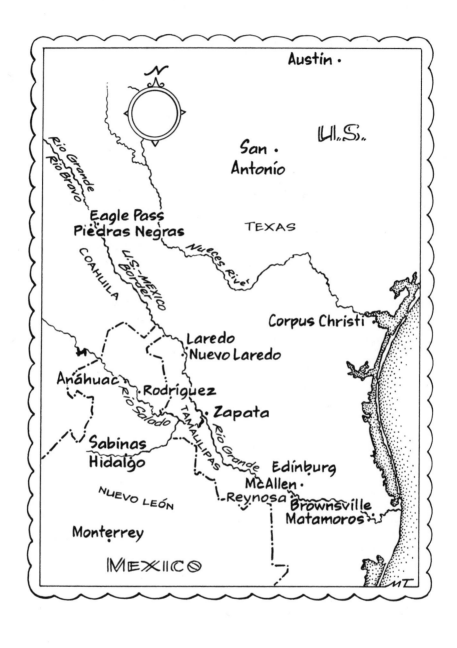

⌁ Introduction ⌁

This work is the second part of a trilogy that goes from the late 1800s to the late 1900s. The first part, *Papeles de Mujer*, consists of correspondence and documents that tell the story of a family in the geographical space between Monterrey, Mexico, and San Antonio, Texas, from 1880 to 1950. That work is entirely in Spanish. The third work is titled *Cabañuelas* and continues the story to the end of the twentieth century. As in most fiction, many of the characters and situations in these three works originate in real people and events, and become fictionalized. In *Canícula*, the story is told through the photographs, and so what may appear to be autobiographical is not always so. On the other hand, many of the events are completely fictional, although they may be true in a historical context. For some of these events, there are photographs; for others, the image is a collage; and in all cases, the result is entirely of my doing. So although it may appear that these stories are my family's, they are not precisely, and yet they are. But then again, as Pat Mora claims, life en la frontera is raw truth, and stories of such life, fictitious as they may be, are even truer than true. I was calling the work fictional autobiography, until a friend suggested that they really are ethnographic and so if it must fit a genre, I guess it is fictional autobioethnography. The *canícula* of the title refers both to the time when I wrote the bulk of the material—the dog days of 1993—and to the idea of a particularly intense part of the summer when most cotton is harvested in South Texas; at that time because of the intense heat, it is said, not even dogs venture out. Canícula: the time between July 14 and August 24, according to my father. In my childhood scheme of things, it is a miniseason that falls between summer and fall. The subtitle merely prepares the reader for what is to come, for this is not a narrative strung out in keeping with Freytag's pyramid: it does not adhere to conventions of plot development. Instead it is a collage of stories gleaned from photographs randomly picked, not from a photo album chronologically arranged, but haphazardly pulled from a box of photos where time is blurred. The story emerges from photographs, photographs through which, as Roland Barthes claimed, the dead return; the stories mirror how we live life in our memories, with our past and our present juxtaposed and bleeding, seeping back and forth, one to the other in a recursive dance.

Norma Elia Cantú

↣ Prologue ↢

In 1980 a car hits a man on a busy Paris street. Roland Barthes dies. The next morning, at the Cafe Colón in Madrid, a woman reads about the accident in *El País* over café con leche and churros. In Paris a few weeks later she buys *Nouvel Observateur* and reads it cover to cover; it's a special issue on Roland Barthes. His book, *Camera Lucida: Reflections on Photography* is published.

In 1980 on the squeaky iron bed in a seventh-floor piso in Madrid two lovers intently go over photographs kept in an old cigar box. Photographs, snapshots, and formal studio photos, yellowing and brittle cover the antique linen bedspread, embroidered and edged with lace. The cigar smell sticks to the photos like the fine dust of time. The woman pieces together her lover's life—the parents smile from black-and-white photos taken before the Spanish Civil War, the war that took the father and left the mother a widow. A baby—cherubic—sits on a manto and gives the camera a wary look; he's an only son. An old girlfriend from England—young, wearing a sweater called a jersey pronounced "hersay" (she's wearing a jersey called a Rebecca after the character in the movie *Rebecca of Sunnybrook Farm*)—her blonde hair very fifties, smiles at the camera, dedicates the photo, "To the one I love." He has offered his life in a sheaf of photos to an intimate stranger from an unknown land he cannot fathom, a land as far from Spain as the unknown, between two countries—Mexico and the United States—a land that's to her as far as last night's dream after listening to *La Traviata* and the dinner he cooked, chicken in red wine sauce, el vino tinto reminding her of her mother's red-blood roses. A land that's to him as far as the moon that waxes in the bluepurple sky above the treetops. She has no photographs to offer, to

1

share her life through. Her photographs, silent witnesses of her life, her history, lie an ocean away, across the Atlantic, across the United States, across Texas, at the borderland where Mexico meets Texas. Her childhood home on San Carlos Street holds the photographs of her life; these are stuffed in shoe boxes tied with old shoelaces, treasured and safe in that land in between that she calls la frontera, the land where her family has lived and died for generations.

In 1985, back in that safe space, between two countries, the woman Nena and her mother bring out the boxes, untie the white-turned-yellow shoelaces, and begin going through the memories. The smell of the past trapped along with the memories. For days, for weeks, for months, they hold the photographs reverently, and the stories come to them. Sometimes the sisters—Dahlia, Esperanza, Azalia, Margarita, Xóchitl—join them and then leave, taking their memories of things, the younger ones not remembering stories, only images, brief descriptions of how they wore a favorite dress; they grieve for a long-past missed birthday, remember a sisterly fight over a long-forgotten childish thing. The father too, curious, interrupts, contributes stories. They continue, the mother filling in gaps for the daughter, of before, of the times before and during that she has forgotten, or changed in her mind—the family, the neighbors, celebrations, events. Some they both experienced yet remember differently; they argue amiably, each sticking to her version of what happened.

The woman Nena begins to shape her story, drawing it out as carefully as when she ripped a seam for her mother, slowly and patiently so the cloth could be resewn without trace of the original seam. The stories of her girlhood in that land in-between, la frontera, are shared; her story and the stories of the people who lived that life with her is one. But who'll hear it?

✍ *Las Piscas* ✍

On a hot, hot, hot August day, the chicharras' drone forces me to the present; they madly hum incessantly, insistently. A long row of cotton to be picked, capullos de algodón, nothing moves; the dust has settled on the green leaves and on my skin. El olor a sudor, mi sudor, heavy odor of sweat I wear with the blue plaid flannel shirt. Can't get away from it. As comforting in its intimacy as Mami's sweet scent of talcum powder and sweat. Sun so bright it hurts my eyes, barely look at it and I see bright red spots. Sweat runs in rivulets along my back. The acrid smell of the pesticide nauseates, sticks to the cushy, dusty white fruit, glassy fibers in my fingers as I pull as carefully as when I pick a burr off my socks. I hold and stash tiny white filaments soft as *barbas de chivo* weed we harvest from Doña Carmen's fence when playing comadritas. Slowly, I fill the saca, custom made by Mami to fit a nine-year-old shoulder. It'll bring fifty cents or even maybe a dollar. Don Guillermo writing it all down in his book when I go with Papi to empty it in the truck. Strange insects—frailesillos, chinches, garrapatas, hormigas—some or all of these pests—ticks, fleas, tiny spiders the color of sand—some or all of these bichos—find their way to exposed ankles, arms, necks and suck life-blood, leaving welts, ronchas—red and itchy—and even pus-filled ampulas that burst and burn with the sun. In the photo, smiles belie tired, aching feet and backs; smiles on serious faces, stiff bodies posed for life. And in the distance the river slithers silently down to the end, or the beginning. High above in the heavens a speck of metal—a jet from the north—flies south, leaves a trail of white cloud as a tail on a homemade paper kite.

⤳ *May* ⤳

Dahlia, Bueli, Tino, cousin Lalo, and I pose one balmy May evening in front of the four-room frame house on San Carlos Street. I and Dahlia wear white organdy—recycled first communion garb. I am all long skinny legs and arms and a flash of white teeth. Later we'll pick flowers— bouquets of tiny pink blossoms, san dieguito; clumps of sweet smelling, ivory-white jasmines, flecks of white on green stems, recedad; bright white daisies we call margaritas; and leafy spiky deep-green ferns, fine as thread—to offer them to Mary at San Luis Rey Church as we sing "O María, Madre mía, o consuelo del mortal, ampararnos y guiarnos a la puerta celestial." And pray the rosary. The smell of incense so strong I want to faint; instead I'll count the lines on the inside of my wrist—each stands for twenty years of my life according to my cousin Pepa. I'll dream of going to Monterrey and eating a pirulí—a candy that really lasts all day long, and you place it in a glass of water overnight so it'll keep. And later after the rosary and the walk and the cup of yerbabuena tea, I lie on

4

the floor out on the porch on a thick colcha and count the stars, sin cuenta! I smile at the joke, *without count* sounding like the number *fifty*—cincuenta—all at once. And maybe wish on a falling star that May will forever be like this.

⤚ Crossings ⤙

Bueli and Mami and Papi crossed the bridge on foot from one Laredo to the other; they took turns carrying me, or maybe only pushing my blue stroller. Chirinola, our dog, came too, papers and all. It was 1948. For Bueli the move brought back memories, mental photographs gone now, except for the stories she told: how in 1935 she and Maurilio, my Texas-born grandfather, and their two young daughters packed all their belongings and drove their pickup truck down from San Antonio. They felt lucky; most deportees left with nothing but the clothes on their back—sent in packed trains to the border on the way to Mexico, even those who were U.S. citizens. She told of crossing from one Laredo to the other and losing everything—Buelito's pride and joy, a black Ford pickup truck and all their belongings—to the corrupt customs officials at the border. Tía Nicha still talks of how weeks later she saw a little girl wearing her dress—a mint green dress she'd hemmed herself with pastel blue thread, a memorable dress so unlike the ugly, drab, navy-blue uniforms of Sacred Heart Elementary School. But there was nothing to be done, except cry and go on. And in 1948 crossing meant coming home, but not quite.

⌁ Rocking Horse ⌁

I ride the rocking horse Buelito's built from discarded wood planks, painted the color of the red coyoles—red as memories. My feet sandaled in brown huaraches from Nuevo Laredo with tiny green nopales and the tinier red pears, tunas, painted on the delicate leather. A white ribbon holds flimsy black curls away from my face; wisps of rebellious curls escape. Mami has made my sundress, blue like the sky, and embroidered tiny pink rosebuds on the handmade smocking—just like the ones she made when she worked as a seamstress at the dress factory. I wear a serious face; riding a horse is serious business at age two. Even as I squint in the noon-time sun, I look straight at the camera at Mami who's kneeling on one knee to be at eye level with me. The screened front door and the window of the house on San Francisco Street where Tino was born frames us, me and my red horse. Blood-red verbena on the ground, tall-leaf co-yoles bloom red in the background. The ride's bumpy on the gravel front yard, but I hold on as tight as if I were riding the real pony I long for—the sad-looking pinto that we ride round and round at the carnival. Because I'm the oldest, I am the beneficiary of Buelito's carpentry skills; he makes toys from wooden spools and toothpicks and rubber bands. Later, when we live on Santa María, the same year Dahlia is born, he'll build a tiny table and chair for me and my dolls. There I'll sit and drink Choco-milk and galletas marías when I come home from Sra. Piña's escuelita where I learn to count and sing and declamar poems for Mother's Day: "Si vieras mamita, que lindas flores / amarillas y azules / de mil colores / aquí las veo abiertas / acá en botón / pero todas alegran mi corazón" and "Un lunes por la mañana me decía mi mamá / levántate, Azucena, si no le digo a tu papá / y yo siendo una niña de carta cabal / me quedaba calladita / '¿Qué no me oyes, lucero? '/ ¿Lucero? si ni candil soy!" Buelito, who is sometimes gone, has come to be with us for awhile. I ride a red rocking horse to the rhythm of lullabyes, look at Mami, and suddenly cry. My tears are round stains on the smock of the pinafore, a darker shade of blue.

◦ On the Bridge ◦

We're crossing the bridge sometime before the flood when the street photographer snaps the picture. Mami holds Esperanza; three of us stand huddled around her. We've been shopping at the Mercado Maclovio Herrera in Nuevo Laredo; we carry bags she calls *redes* full of meat, sugar, tomatoes, groceries. Papi's gone to work in construction and only comes home once a month. Sometimes, she sends Tino and me to run these errands. We make the rounds at the mercado, go to the butcher's and buy red juicy meat and have it ground by Raúl who winks as he puts in a pilón; we go to Rangel's for cookies—galletas marías and morenas—and sugar, piloncillo, and dark aguacates which he carefully cuts in half, satisfying U.S. Department of Agriculture requirements he extracts the pit so we can legally cross them to the United States and closes them again, like fine carved wood boxes. We carefully count out the money, figuring out the exchange pesos to dollars. Tino gets a shoeshine at the plaza across from Santo Niño de Atocha Church; I eat fruit—perhaps a slice of watermelon, pineapple, or jícama—sprinkled with red chili powder; we drink jamaica from tall glasses, the red thirst-quencher fills my bladder; I must go. At the Mercardo Maclovio Herrera baths I stand in line, crossing one leg over the other as I stand and wait, about to burst; the old woman who sits by the toilets carefully cuts thin brownish tissue paper; hands it to me, I hand her a veinte, a Mexican coin brown and fat. Ritualized exchange. The smell of disinfectant can't disguise the other smell, stronger and overpowering, that lies underneath, makes me want to gag; I hurry. Come out to the blinding, shining sunlight. We walk, cross the bridge, resting every half block or so, resting our arms, sore from carrying the heavy redes. We take the bus home.

In the photo Mami squints in the sun, she is beautiful and angry, impatient. The weight of all of us on her shoulders. Soon, Papi quits the construction job with Zachry Construction. Too many nights away from home, working in strange cities called Waco and Odessa. Buys an old grey Nash that looks like a giant water bug, the headlights two puffy eyes. He finds work at the smelter where Tío Güero and Antonio, our neighbor, work, and with them will be laid off periodically. During those times the trips to Laredo, Mexico, are put on hold; only for emergencies do we cross—to see the doctor, to visit an ill relative, or to pay a manda at Santo Niño de Atocha Church. Tino and I miss our adventures, our sojourns al otro lado. Now Papi takes Tino to get haircuts and shoes shined while Mami and I buy *Confidencias*, a women's magazine I'll read a escondidas, during siesta time. Hiding in the backyard, under the pirul,

8

I'll read "Cartas que se extraviaron," and pretend the love letters are for me, or that I wrote them, making the tragic stories mine. I pretend I'm a leading star—María Félix, Miroslava, Silvia Pinal. During recess, I retell the stories to Sanjuana and Anamaría, embellishing to fit my plots.

⌁ The Flood ⌁

A scary flood, threatening and overwhelming. The massive bridge, wiped away as if it were a matchstick toy like the ones Buelito makes for me. And the people gather in the streets, the men home from the smelter, the factory, the store because of the disaster. Salinases, Mendozas, Treviños, Bacas, Valdezes and Sánchezes, all have gathered in our front yard. We fear disaster. But as they listen to the radio—to the announcers talking on and on all afternoon—the fear becomes commonplace. Late into the night we play "a la roña," chasing each other—the adults don't seem to care if we stay up. We are ready to evacuate; clothes and a few possessions packed in pillowcases, in boxes, in paper sacks, we wait. Finally, the word comes: Zacate Creek is rising; we must leave and go to the high school gym on San Bernardo for the night. And we sleep safe and sound, exhausted by waiting, playing, fearing. The next day we come home. The flood without rain has come and gone. Back home, we find the water stopped at our doorstep. Our homes are safe, for they sit high on stilts. But the raging water took what it could: our stairs, the mailbox; it up-rooted peach trees, but the orange and grapefruit trees held on, as did the mesquite, the huisache, and the pirul, the pirul struck by lightning only three years later. Mami's roses, her hibiscus we know as tulipanes, the jasmine, recedad, the ferns are all gone.

Later, we brave a bridge that swings, made of wood and rope, to cross the river to check on friends and family who, not so fortunate as we, have lost their house, their furniture, everything to the cleansing, avenging waters. Bueli prays other prayers, not just the usual, "Vente Azucena, no

9

te quedes," and I, wanting to assure her that I'm not staying with the river spirits, repeat as if chanting, "ay voy, ay voy, ay voy" as we cross the river, going and coming. The toy bridge swinging, and I holding on to Bueli as she prays. Now we fear illness, typhoid, crippling polio, some because of the flood, others whose origins are mysterious. So we wait for hours and hours standing in line for immunization shots and for water and for more immunization shots that hurt. Most kids cry, but I am courageous, shut my eyes tight to keep from crying; my brother follows my lead and tears come, but he doesn't scream, but Dahlia runs and runs, all over the grounds around the high school, crying, wanting to escape the inevitable, embarrassing us all. Mami's fears multiply with the stories of kids who get polio and fevers so severe they kill. Bueli lights candles to the image of the Virgen de San Juan by her bed—the one that glows silvery in the dark and is grey over old rose in the light of day. One Sunday morning we pile into Compadre Leo's car. Before the sun's even up, we're on our way to the shrine for the Virgen in San Juan, down in the Valley, to thank the Virgen for sparing our house. The photo shows five adults— Mami, Papi, Leo, Tina, Bueli—and five children standing before Compadre Leo's Ford. We come home late that night, tired and sweaty. I pretend to sleep. When Bueli tries to wake me, I make myself heavy until Compadre Leo carries me in, lays me on the bed. "She's a seven-year-old baby," I hear Mami say.

After the flood, Mami and Bueli begin again, all year they plant, sharing cuttings from neighbors' plants that have survived: hibiscus, jasmines, ferns and roses, and a brand new gardenia bush right under the bedroom window to sweeten the night air. And Bueli's herbs—ruda for earaches, albahcar, estafiate for fevers, romero, and yerbabuena for everything. The store where our neighbor Don Vicente works, only a block from the bridge, is ruined. Soon, only watermarks on the walls of banks, stores, offices, reminders of loss, of fear, remain along with photographs from the newspaper like the one Mami has saved along with her photos.

⌁ Pepa ⌁

At my cousin Pepa's quinceañera they serve chicken in mole, a rich chocolaty sauce, and I try to be neat, but it's impossible. And there I am, a wisp of a girl, smiling at the camera, my arms strategically crossed trying to hide red-brown mole spots on my pastel yellow dress, a hand-me-down from Chelito, Mami's friend who lives in Corpus Christi. Pepa's hand rests on my shoulder, and I know I'm her favorite cousin. My best friend Anamaría claims Pepa's not really my cousin, claims that Tía Trine and my uncle never married. But, I don't care, she's still my favorite. She paints my nails with red, red polish; combs, braids, curls my hair. She was there to comfort me when Mami pierced my ears, strung red floss, then placed tiny gold loops through the needlewide holes. She treats me like a little sister, wants me next to her on the photo taken in their backyard. The smell of orange blossoms intoxicating, drawing the bees that Quico, Pepa's youngest brother teases. They sting him; he cries. But no sound comes forth until he turns purple and finally lets out a scream that brings everyone to him. Everyone has remedies: cobwebs, no that's for cuts; mud, no that's for insect bites, well, maybe; ice-cubes; mashed rue; aloe vera. But, Tía Trine will have none of that and scolds him and tells him he deserves it for playing with bees. Soon he's playing with the rest of us; after all it was only two bees that got him. But now he cautiously plays on the other side of the yard by the fig tree and away from the orange trees. At the dinner, Dahlia cries and screams: she wants a grownup plate. Mami's embarrassed, but Tía Trine brings a plate just like the adults' with jalapeños and all, sets it before two-year-old Dahlia on the picnic table, and she's happy. Later, she'll cry and scream again to see Mami and Papi dancing to Isidro López on the record player. Mami excuses Dahlia's crankiness saying, "She's just chípil." And it's true, Mami's pregnant. Esperanza comes soon after that.

⌁ Esperanza ⌁

It's a cold January night. I've laid out my clothes for school. Said my prayers, made the sign of the cross over my pillow three times like Bueli has taught me. In the middle of the night I awaken to commotion and crying. "It's okay," Bueli calms me, "it's only the cats fighting." I go back to sleep. In the morning, I'm surprised Mami's not in the kitchen, but still in bed. Bueli's making tortillas and chorizo con huevo for breakfast, she's fixing Papi's lunchbox. "There's a surprise for you, a new sister," Papi says and takes a sip of coffee. In the bed, a tiny little bundle. A baby no bigger than Gatón, my cat, suckles at Mami's breast. I'm fascinated, full of questions. By now I know that babies aren't bought at the store like when I was trained to say that I was bought at the Mercado Maclovio Herrera in Nuevo Laredo and Tino at Kress's in Laredo. But all Mami will say is Carlota came in the night and brought this real live doll with her. Carlota who comes and sits under the pirul, talking while Bueli and Mami quilt. Carlota who laughs so loud I think she's crying. How? Why? I don't want to go to school, especially when Carlota, the partera, arrives to check on Mami and the baby. I want to carry the baby, bathe her, wake her up, teach her to talk, sing her to sleep as I swing the cradle. But I have to go to school, where I brag about my new baby sister. A few months later, it's no fun at all to rinse her diapers, burying the mustard yellow mass that stinks worse than rotten eggs and makes my stomach want to come up. I run the tap water straight onto the soiled area, and then pile the diapers into a pail with bleach. Mami or Bueli will boil them in a washtub, set on bricks over a fire, stir them with an old broomstick. Rinse them in another tub. I help, too: hang each diaper, clean-smelling of bleach, on the line with wooden pins a challenge to open for my seven-year-old hands. And I bring them in and fold them before the evening dew comes. The same sereno that heals mouth sores can give the baby a rash.

Only a few days after she arrives, the new baby gets sick and is dying one night. "She's leaving us," Bueli cries. She's having convulsions, has turned purple. Papi's working the night shift or maybe is working out of town, I feel his absence as fear. Juanita, Mamagrande's entenada, is visiting and offers remedios that don't work. Scared, Mami sends me to Jovita's to use the phone, call a doctor, explain. It's dark and they don't hear my frantic knocking. Pita, their dog wags her tail, greets me with a whine and a cold nose on my bare leg. I use a rock, bang against the screen, the door shut against the cold. Still no answer. I call, "Jovita!" and finally Eusebio hears the Valdez's dogs barking next door and comes to the door, turns on the light, and sees me. I make the call. The doctor speaks English. My words come out in Spanish. I'm terrified, but I understand: she wants the baby in the hospital. Now. Eusebio takes Mami, Esperanza, and Juanita to the hospital. The nurses, the doctor, all are sure she's going to die. Juanita becomes her emergency room madrina as they baptize the three-day-old baby. Mami offers her to the statue of St. Joseph in the waiting room at Mercy Hospital. That's why she's "Esperanza José," the only one with a middle name. The infant so weak and limp she wouldn't even cry is soon screaming for her food, responding to the medicine, surprising everyone. She survives, and comes home. And Juanita, raised by Mamagrande when her own mother died of tuberculosis, becomes Espy's madrina. Eleazar, my neighbor and friend, sits with me under the mesquite, talking. He angers me to tears with his questions: what will we do if the baby dies, what if the illness comes back and she dies? They'll have to bury her, just like they buried her ombligo in the backyard near the mesquite tree, and I remember Papi burying the dark mass, that finally fell leaving a neat belly button on the baby's tummy. I'm furious, I won't play or talk with him for days. And Tía Nicha asks who's my favorite, and I say Esperanza, of course. Why? Well, because, she is. That's all.

Easter 1952

ᕁ *Tino* ᕁ

He did it at four. And again at nine. He stands to the side with his hand out as if pointing a gun or a rifle. Everyone else is crowded around me; the piñata in the shape of a birthday cake sways in the wind above our heads. Everyone's there: aunts, uncles, cousins, the neighbors, my madrina, everyone, even Mamagrande Lupita from Monterrey. I'm holding the stick decorated with red, blue, yellow tissue paper that we will use to break the piñata. And he's playing, even in the picture, at being a soldier. Only ten years later, 1968, he is a soldier, and it's not a game. And we are gathered again: tías, tíos, cousins, comadres, neighbors, everyone, even Mamagrande Lupita from Monterrey, and Papi's cousin Ricardo who's escorted the body home. We have all gathered around a flag-draped coffin. Tino's come home from Vietnam. My brother. The sound of the trumpet caresses our hearts and Mami's gentle sobbing sways in the cool wind of March.

↶ Perpetuo Socorro ↷

On the wall, the image of the Virgen de San Juan, a pale rose background, grayish black outline, shines like silver in the dark. Bueli lights candles when Tino is so sick el Doctor del Valle, the doctor in Laredo, Mexico, fears he will die. He's only three. The illness has taken over. But Papi cries in front of another image of our Lady. It's a calendar from Cristo Rey Church with the image of Nuestra Señora del Perpetuo Socorro. He prays, he weeps, hits the wall with his fists, like he would hit the mesquite tree in the backyard with his head sixteen years later like a wounded animal, mourning, in pain, that morning when Tino's death came to our door. But the child Tino survives the illness; the injections, the medication, the prayers, the remedios—something works, and Papi frames the calendar image in gold leaf, builds the image a repisita—a shelf for candles. In 1968, in his pain, tears running down his face, he'll talk to the image, "For this, you spared my son," he'll take the image down from its place on the wall, cannot bear to see it, to be reminded. On the wall, a rectangle of nothing, the color of the wallpaper Mami had hung for Tío Moy's last visit three years ago, like new—lines of green fern leaves on dusty beige. The votive candle on the tiny shelf still burning to an empty space.

↶ Papi's Horse ↷

My father is on his favorite horse. He wears a hat that casts a shadow over his face, but I can tell he's smiling his "I'm-so-proud-smile." He's young in the photo, it must be in Allende or in one of the nearby ranches where he grew up. In the photo, a huge cedar ash windbreaker sepia-darkens one side of the jacal in the background where a field extends into the sky. The land. My father venerates it, even now as he grows a couple of corn plants, squash, tomatoes. He used to talk of going back to Mexico, of settling in a small town, Vallecillo, Sabinas, Anáhuac. "A ranchito, to plant again," he'd say. He doesn't mention these plans any more, resigned to arthritic disability, to retirement in Laredo. When we drove to the places where he'd lived as a child the trajectory went from Nuevo Laredo to Anáhuac, Rodríguez, Allende, Piedras Negras— through three Mexican states—Tamaulipas, Nuevo León, Coahuila, all in a day. And he joked about not visiting Las Minas, the mining town of Dolores, Texas, where he'd been conceived.

He tells his grandsons about his favorite horse, the one he'd ride to dances far and wide around Anáhuac, and how he had to shoot the horse he named Rocinante. The stories of the dances invariably lead to the stories about Gonzalo. Gonzalo, the brother who came back from California with the Model T, who loved to dance and tell jokes. In a teary voice he tells how his oldest brother was killed at a dance, at a ranch wedding, defending a friend, how he held him and wept as the uncle I never met breathed his last. And Papagrande would not have revenge and forbade his sons to seek it. My father was but sixteen and his older brother died at thirty-two, leaving two widows, one in Texas and the other in Mexico. At the wake both showed up and Mamagrande was beside herself with grief—and embarrassment. ¡Qué dirá la gente! But no one could deny Tía Trine her mourning. She brought her child to see her dead father and to meet her half-siblings. Defying Papagrande, she stood and received "el pésame" with the rest of the family. And my father rode his Rocinante, and let his moustache grow in memory of his brother, the moustache that darkened as he grew into manhood and has whitened as he has aged into our lives.

⌐ Mamagrande ⌐

The photo shows a woman sitting surrounded by children—they're her sons and daughters, grandsons and granddaughters. Mamagrande, after the move south, she of the blue blood, living in Anáhuac, the house at the parcela, not quite fit for her. Her aquamarine eyes behind gold-framed eyeglasses fill with tears that she dries with beautifully embroidered handkerchiefs. Mamagrande tells me stories of crossing the river "en wayin"—and I imagine a covered wagon like in the movies—and she pregnant with my Dad. Papagrande, the pacifist, made the decision and she followed south, as she had before fleeing the revolution in Mexico, going north to Las Minas, the area of the coal mines—Chanel, Dolores, Palafox. Now they flee again, when men they know who don't speak English are drafted, sent to fight overseas. World War I has come and they're moving again. Papagrande herding the goats, the younger children packed into the wagon, the older ones on horseback, crossing the river to Mexico once again. She holds her dreams in her heart. In the photo the tired woman almost lost among the children. The work, endless. From cooking daily meals—sopa de arroz, guisados, postres for lunch—and fancy festive meals—cabrito, mole, tamales—to keeping the linens whiter than white, fighting the dust and the grime of life on a ranch of a town. The keeping up of appearances, of dignity, of what is right is even more tiring. She yearns for the carefree girl she was, her girlhood house in the town near Monterrey where her ancestors settled newly come from Spain, yearns for servants to launder, iron fine linens, and the pleasures of her girl-life, Mass on Sundays and squash candy or yams with milk and honey. She married at fifteen, she tells me. "When I was your age, I'd birthed two children." Her parents buried in the family crypt in the main cemetery in Monterrey. Her children buried in Nuevo Laredo, in Dolores, in Anáhuac. Her pains and her joys buried in her heart, her hands ever busy crocheting, embroidering, knitting, quilting. The work never stops, her handkerchief a la mano in her apron pocket ever ready for the tears of joy or of pain. Mamagrande.

17

ᜡ Los Pulido ᜡ

Only four of the sixteen stand shyly in our front porch. Socorro, Leonor, Toño, Irene. Sofía, Mercedes, Fidel, Elena, Lucía, Clementina, Patricia, Javier, Sara, Emilio, Josefina, and Cecilia: names of eight born in Mexico and then the other eight born in the States. A family Comadre Fina wouldn't have imagined as a child growing up in the Anglo-owned ranch near Big Wells, Texas. But such is life; "así es la vida," she would exclaim, sitting under the pirul chatting with Mami, her comadre. She was U.S.-born and married to a real Mexican macho who wooed her back to Mexico with promises of wealth. Wouldn't leave his mother's side when Comadre Fina gave him the ultimatum—she pregnant with her ninth, Lucía, who lived only three years. Así es la vida. No, he didn't come join her in the United States until Lucía died; his own mother died a month after his daughter. Four of them, the Pulidos, in the faded black-and-white picture, I can't even tell who they are. But Pulido they are; "borrados" we called them because of their light skin and hazel eyes. In the photo they grin shyly, and I feel their embarrassment; the other kids tease them and call them "mojados" because they are new to the neighborhood, although they have come from Big Wells and not directly from Mexico. The same kids called mojados by the white kids pick on them. They will soon leave to work the fields in the Midwest—Nebraska, Wisconsin, Michigan—only to return in the fall, way after school has begun. Years later, after the older ones marry, they'll move to California, change their migrant route and travel only in that state, following the crops, buy a piece of land in the middle of an orange grove near Fresno. Así es la vida. But while still our neighbors, they have corn tortilla tacos with beans for breakfast—so unlike our own flour tortillas filled with papas con huevo. Still, we all drink the same café con leche Pet each morning before going to school.

↜ Dahlia One ↝

It's Dahlia's first birthday; that very same day she learns to walk. We've gathered around a piñata for a photograph. In the background a cubreviento—the one that tells me stories about birds and frogs, until I find out trees don't talk. We live in a barrio called Cantarranas, and on those rare nights when thunder lights up the night sky and the rains come, Bueli tells us about La Llorona, for if one listens very carefully, in the midst of the crying of the frogs one can almost hear the wailing of a woman looking for her children along the river banks. The story never varies and sometimes I fall asleep before Bueli ends with "colorín colorado éste cuento se ha acabado." But other times I am full of questions left unanswered by the story and by Bueli, who teases me calling me a lawyer always full of questions. She embellishes the story, but she never answers my questions: why would she kill her own children? Why would she then cry for them? Why, if she lived by the river, didn't we ever see her? Were there other children? How many were there? What were their ages, their names?—none of that matters—the tale never answers my questions.

A while later. I must be five, for I have forgotten the language of trees, we have moved to Las Cruces, a barrio farther away from the river, and La Llorona now wails along Zacate Creek a couple of blocks behind our new home—a small four-room frame house built on stilts. She's still looking for her lost children—my mother tells me—so I am never to go near the creek; La Llorona might mistake me for one of her lost children and take me with her, and I must also watch and make sure my younger siblings don't go near the water either. La Llorona, a bedtime tale, Bueli would tell her wide-eyed grandchildren on the rare rainy nights in Laredo in a barrio named Cantarranas, singing frogs along the banks of the Rio Grande, Rio Bravo. In the photo, Dahlia who has taken her very first steps, smiles a toothless grin, I hold her pudgy one-year-old hand in mine; La Llorona is far away, as Bueli, wearing her good dress, the blue one with tiny white flowers all over, holds my hand.

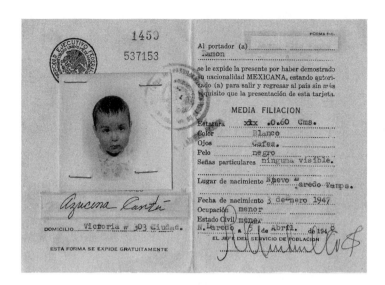

ᔕ Mexican Citizen ᔐ

In the photo stapled to my official U.S. immigration papers, I am a one-year-old baldy, but the eyes are the same that stare back at me at thirteen when I look in the mirror and ask "Who am I?" and then go and cut my hair standing there in front of the mirror, just like Mia Farrow's in Peyton Place; Papi has a fit. The eyes are the same as the ones on another photo where I am twelve—this one stapled to a document that claims I am a Mexican citizen so I can travel with Mamagrande into Mexico without my parents. We sit for hours waiting at the consulado on Farragut Street until our number is called and the cheery clerk talks to Mamagrande, takes the papers to a mysterious back room to have the cónsul sign, and finally returns. The papers flourishingly signed and decorated with an official stamp—I am declared a Mexican national. I can travel back to Mexico without my parents. I stare into the camera a shy skinny twelve-year-old anxious about body hair and developing breasts that seem to be growing

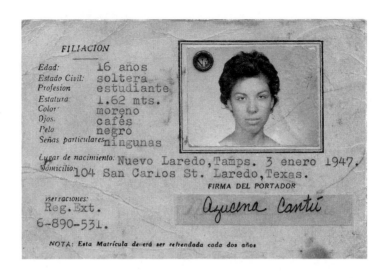

out one larger than the other. Anamaría my best friend confides that that is her fear, too, for as oldest sisters we have been carrying babies almost all our short lives; since December we've been consciously shifting the babies from the right to the left so we won't have one breast larger than the other. We marvel at the bras hung on the line every Monday morning at the Valdezes', Doña Cata must have huge breasts, even bigger than Doña Carmen's, whose bras we've never seen on her line, so we deduce she doesn't wear a bra. We're obsessed by breasts, daily checking our self-perceived asymmetrical protuberances. And talk of when we'll wear bras and how to ask our mothers for bras for next year: how can we go back to eighth grade braless? Such a tragedy! Such a dilemma! But now I'm off to Monterrey with Mamagrande, to her house on Washington Street across from the Alameda. Where my cousins will tease me and call me *pocha* and make me homesick for my U.S. world full of TV—Ed Sullivan and Lucy and Dinah Shore and Lawrence Welk, Bueli's favorite—and Glass Kitchen hamburgers—eight, then six for a dollar on Saturday afternoons. I'm homesick for parents, and siblings, and bingo at San Luis Rey Church with Concha our neighbor. Cousins. Kind and cruel, ask me to say something in English, I recite, "I pledge allegiance to the flag . . . ;" to sing something, and I sing to them silly nursery rhymes and tell them these are great songs: Humpty Dumpty, Jack and Jill, Little Miss Muffet, Old MacDonald. They listen fascinated, awed, but then they laugh when I don't know their games, "A la víbora, víbora de la mar, de la mar," or their hand-clapping games, "Yo no soy bonita ni lo quiero ser, porque las bonitas se echan a perder." And, "Padre e hija fueron a misa, se encontraron un francés . . ." I'm homesick and I don't have a word for it—I cry silently at night asleep in a cot out on the zaguán of the long long house with the colonial windows that face the street, sills close to the floor, cool to the touch, so wide we play jacks on them while the adults sleep their siesta. Cousins. Tina, Lupana, Tati. Scare me with stories of robachicos who steal children and sell them as slaves, or make them beg at the entrance of the cathedral. Cousins. Pita. Chabela. Rey. Teach me to ride a bicycle, to barter with the vendors, and I laugh at their jokes even when I don't understand them. Cousins. I'm sent as chaperone to Tina. She meets Chago, a escondidas. Later, at home, in my innocence I let it out that Chago bought me a paleta—de mango, my favorite—and she really gets it. Papagrande fuming; they don't like Chago because he's not Catholic, in fact he's the son of a Protestant minister. But I don't care. I like his laughing hazel eyes and curly puppy-brown hair. The next day on the way to Felita's to pick up an "encargo" for Mamagrande, Tina explains. I must learn to keep secrets otherwise Papagrande will be angry. I listen and obey, learn the lessons of growing up.

↫ *Bueli* ↬

In the photo, Bueli sits in her high-back rocking chair, her sillón where she'd rocked all of us to sleep, surrounded by Tino, Dahlia, Esperanza, and me, in our nine-by-nine living room with the pseudo pink lace plastic curtains, her hair braided and wrapped on her head like a crown, adorned with grey plastic combs, my Mother's Day gift from Kress's where I spent thirty minutes and thirty cents deciding on just this pair with the encrusted rhinestones. Because we crowd into the small room, wanting to be in the picture, Mami takes it at an odd angle; Espy's two-year-old face looms huge in the foreground. On the wall, hangs the calendar from San Luis Rey Church. In the very same room, we prayed around her coffin. The night she was buried I saw her. She sat rocking back and forth on her sillón in the living room. She told me to take care of the baby. With-

24

out words she spoke, "Cuida la niña," and I understood she meant Azalia, only three months old. I get up and check—she's asleep in the cradle Papi had painted the color of eggnog and decorated with bunny decals. Azalia's fine. But Mami's crying. We both cry, hug. When I tell her what Bueli said, Mami instructs, "Pray so her spirit can be at peace." And I do.

↶ Azalia ↷

Tino and I argue over what to watch on TV. There's only two channels— one from Laredo in English and one from Nuevo Laredo in Spanish. It's Saturday before school starts. Mami and Papi have gone to get our school clothes, shoes, supplies—Big Chief tablets for the little ones, loose-leaf paper and binders for the older ones, satchels and yellow pencils for all of us. Everything had been put on layaway weeks before. Mami has been paying on the accounts at Neisner's and J. C. Penney's every week. Luckily we've been working in the fields and she hasn't missed a week. Six-month-old Azalia squirms in my arms as Tino and I struggle, switching the knob back and forth. Azalia gentle and quiet as always, "Muñeca," Papi's nickname for her. Suddenly I lose my hold on her, she's falling and I'm still holding her legs. She cries and cries.

"See, what you did!"

"Nothing. I didn't do it." And we forget the TV for a while.

"Espy, get me some sugar, for her susto," I order Esperanza.

I coo, sing all the lullabies I know, rocking and praying. Nothing works. Not even the camomile tea I fix with plenty of honey. Finally she falls asleep in my arms, puffy, red-cheeked from crying, sighing for a long time even in her sleep. When I lay her down, she cries a little but settles down when I swing the cuna, and hum a lullaby, "Señora santana, porqué llora Lala, por una manzana que se le perdió . . ." Mami and Papi come in loaded with the things we had picked out weeks before, new shoes and clothes, school supplies. But the things are never as nice as we remember. The baby Azalia fidgets and cries but doesn't wake up until morning. When Mami notices she's not moving one leg, and that she cries and cries, I tell her what happened. It's Sunday, and they take her to the emergency room. The baby Lala comes back with a fat white cast on her leg. For weeks she'll bang on the cuna enjoying the thump, thump, thump of the cast against the wooden frame. The doctor hopes the break will heal without causing permanent damage. But we won't know till she's fifteen or eighteen, she says. Guilt ridden, I agonize for years, and it's not until Azalia's a high school cheerleader and I see her cartwheel across the track, and jump and dance as she cheers the Tiger football team that the susirio lifts from my soul. At her wedding, I pray, "See, Bueli, I did take care of her."

⌁ Ojo de Agua ⌁

In the black-and-white photo taken by Papi at the ojo de agua in Sabinas, a lanky teen smiles into the sun, shoulder-length hair caught blowing in the breeze. I'm wearing my cousin Tina's hand-me-down dress, a bright green cotton sateen, one with the three-quarter length sleeves, the wide collar, and side-zipper that always got stuck. It's a handmade dress and one of my favorites. The wide belt with the cloth-covered buckle reminds me of a dress Audrey Hepburn wears in *Roman Holiday* or some such movie I saw many years later, for at that time we only saw Mexican movies at the Cine Azteca or Cine México in Laredo or at the theaters in Nuevo Laredo. I wear black patent-leather, pointy-toe shoes Tía Luz bought for me and which I know my father disapproves of. I'm not dressed for a picnic, but then, this was an impromptu one; we've stopped to rest during the hottest time of the day and we'll soon be on our way. It's so hot that I feel the heat rising from the stones; I stand on a stone as large as a giant turtle's back and the heat penetrates the thin soles of my grown-up shoes. Papi has called me away from the shady avocado trees loaded with fruit along the banks where I was wading in the cool spring water, where the youngest of my siblings happily splash and play in their underwear. My shoulder-length hair curls with the humidity, curly wisps frame my face. There's a sadness in my eyes that's hard to understand. We're on our way back from Monterrey where I've spent the better half of summer as Mamagrande's spoiled pocha granddaughter. I've been enjoying my cousins—Pita and Chabela who are younger and Tati who's my age, we've gone to movies with our "domingo" and "helped" by selling chickens from Tía Lucita's granja to the city neighbors—glad I wasn't older because the older cousins Tina and Lupana had to submerge the freshly killed chickens in boiling hot water and pluck them clean. I don't know this, but this is the next to the last summer that I'll go there. It is different, I feel grown up; I've started hanging out at the Alameda not like a child in the playground, but on Sunday evenings, platicando with boyfriends that change each week, but not really boyfriends. I'm sad to leave that world, but excitedly anticipate going to Lamar Junior High and resuming friendships with Nancy, my gringa friend whose family's stationed at Laredo Air Force Base, and Marilu, my friend from elementary, and Helen, my pachuca friend whose nickname is Toro, and Chelito—no, Chelito won't be there, in my absence she's gotten married or so the cryptic note from Estér claims. Later I will discover that she eloped with Tony who's almost eight years older and they've gone to Houston to live with his cousin, Cefe. She's only fourteen. I'm scared, at the same time curious: what's it like to be married? To leave? Papi clicks the Brownie; the kids squeal in the background. An urraca perched on a dead branch caws, sounds just like Cande, Mamagrande's neighbor, when she calls out to her kids—Caro, Chole, Tano, vengan! Mami proclaims that the weather will soon change. I'm aware of the adult talk, the water, feel the heat below and above me, but I only hear the black bird's warning; shivers run up my spine.

27

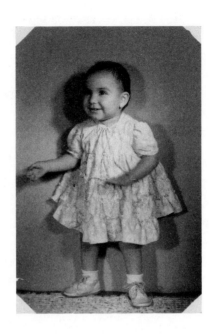

ᴧ First Steps ᴧ

I'm about to take a step—on my first birthday, bald, wide-eyed, and chunky, wearing a handmade pale pink satin dress Mami embroidered with beautiful smocking on afternoons that fall of 1947 when my father had gone al norte to Gary, Indiana, with her cousins Meme, Abelardo, and Moy to find work. He'd been working as a baker with his brother-in-law in Nuevo Laredo. Decided to chance it up north where they said one could get rich. The bakery didn't have a future, or rather, he didn't have a future with the bakery. Papi didn't last up there in that cold, harsh place, where everything was the color of cement grey and sad, where he could only speak with Mami's family and co-workers. Everywhere the English sounds, like the sounds of an unfamiliar engine that he couldn't decipher, frustrated him. Claims he never thought of anything except coming home. The minute he got there, all he wanted was to come home. And as soon as he'd paid off the contractor and saved enough money to move us to the United States, he rushed home to us. Came home that spring of '48, determined, ready to make the move to the U.S. side, but not too far north, not too far away from family. Mami talks of loving the time alone with Bueli, the sewing time, making clothes for me on long lonely afternoons and evenings. It's my birthday and Mami's having a real photographer take the picture to send to him so far away in a place so cold snow falls from the sky and turns everything white. Mamagrande's gift, a gold chain with a gold medal of her namesake, our Lady of Guadalupe, around my neck, a gold bracelet on my wrist. I'm about to take a step.

ᕈ Third Grade ᕈ

Third Grade. Saunders School May celebration and I am the master of ceremonies, recruited only the day before because Griselda, the fourth grader who was chosen emcee is sick. I am terrified that I will forget the memorized welcome speech. "Don't worry," Mrs. Treviño instructs, "if you forget here's the talk in your pocket, just pull it out and read it." And of course in the middle of my talk, when I look up and see the sea of faces, Mami's amongst them, I do forget and I pull out the "papelito," and everyone laughs, but I pretend not to notice and I continue, on tiptoe, reading the welcome speech into the microphone that is too high for me. Because I'm performing, too, I have to rush and change while the second graders dance. Then the third graders are on: we dance to "Mr. Sandman," not knowing what it's all about we prance around: Angelita, Helen, Marilu, Anamaría, Peewee, and I. I'm in pajamas, a flowery pink and green print Mami's sewn especially for today. As we bow, the applause sends warm shivers all over. In the photo the six of us with pillows for props. When my part of the emceeing is over, I go down and sit with friends. Later, Fito and Nacho chase us around the back of the makeshift auditorium. When the adults quiet us down and we're sitting on the floor in front of the stage, Dahlia reaches over and bites Fito's arm leaving red and purple teeth marks—he cries and cries and Cuqita his mother tells Mami that if he gets sick we'll see. Mami gets after me for not taking better care of Dahlia. Tino says he'll get Fito for being such a cry baby.

⤙ Políticos ⤚

It may be September, when rains come down so hard they almost flood our house, even though it's built on stilts. The rains are gone, only the hot sun and the puffy clouds like cotton, high up in the sky, remain. Eisenhower visits Laredo, and we line Saunders Street to see a convertible speeding by from the airbase to the bridge. A gringo waving to the brown faces of all ages that have come to see him. "¡Viva Ike!" someone shouts. But, he doesn't hear; doesn't seem to see us waving in the hot morning sun. When Miss Montemayor asks if anyone knows who the president is, I raise my hand, impress my teacher, "Eisenhower, and the vice president is Nixon, but we don't like them; they're not Democrats." Repeating in English what I've heard in Spanish at home. And Mami and Papi sacrifice to pay their poll tax, then give their vote to their compadre who works for the city so he won't get fired. At twenty-one I'll still ask why and rebel, and won't give my vote to the machine. Papi shrugs, "We'd vote Democrat, anyway. And this way if the smelter lays off again, I may get a job with the county." I don't understand. Remain angry at the machine, the bosses who control, who deprive. The políticos. Our money lines their pockets, paves private roads on their ranches, while our streets remain unpaved, run like rivers after every rain, while our public library remains as small as someone's private library; while the dropout rate remains between 50 and 80 percent; while judges, mayors,

30

sheriffs, high and low powerful ones abuse, rape, embarrass, harass, taunt, demean women. I see the pain, the hopelessness, the survival strategies of the poor. At eighteen, I can't forgive. At eight I ponder what makes men so important. That year, because I know their names, I make good grades in social studies and in English, I get to have my picture in the paper with Mr. Valle the principal who speaks our names in English— Murreea, Anjeleeta, calls me "Nina" instead of "Nena." We arrive in his Buick, meet the superintendent and the photographer who proceeds to line us up on the stairs in front of the main office on Victoria Street. Soon sweat runs down Superintendent Nixon's red face. Sweat beads into droplets on Mr. Valle's balding head. Some years later, both are dead; other men have taken their place. And I march to Austin protesting with the farmworkers; march in rallies protesting Vietnam; march for the ERA; wonder what else I can do, a lowly office clerk; wear a César Chávez button, read Marx.

⌒ Nacho ⌒

Nacho had sent the stone flying through the air in my direction; I'd skirted it, making him even angrier. But as it hit the ground next to me, the truth hit me hard, like the stone hit the ground—it was true. I liked him and he liked me. Why was I so upset then that I took careful aim and, anticipating where he would run, sent the stone flying and hit him right on the arm? I could hear him crying all the way home. Mami was incredulous when Nacho and his Mom showed up at our front porch to complain and make sure that I got punished. His Mom was red-angry and kept calling me a "malcriada," and a "bandida." I was mortified and blushed and blushed and couldn't even defend myself until they were gone and I couldn't hold the tears any longer. "But, Mami, he tried to hit me first. Chata's my witness," I told her. "You can ask her, she'll tell you how the others were teasing us; we were playing bebeleche. I only threw

31

the stone, the one I was using as my 'prenda,' after he almost hit me."
How could I tell Mami of the anger, the humiliation, the mixed-up feelings that were held in that stone and in me? She'd never understand. I
took my punishment, but already I was plotting revenge. I was going to
write him a poem, call him a chimuelo chismoso; that'd serve him right.
I savored the joy of having everyone laugh at him, as I read the poem
at recess.

✕ Cowgirl ✕

In the photograph, Peewee, Angelita, Sanjuana, and I wear long red-checked dresses; I smile a toothless second-grader chimuela—grin. And holding Quico's hand, I pose in front of the blackboard with the alphabet running across the top, with the U.S. flag we pledged allegiance to every morning. Right hand over the heart—I was always getting it wrong; although I wasn't zurda—it still felt "right" to pledge with the left hand not the right. We were to dance a sort of square dance for the end-of-the-year program. My brand-new, black patent shoes, bought with the money Mami made selling dresses she sewed on Bueli's Singer, remain hidden by the long, full skirt of the red gingham dress, also one of Mami's creations. My black curly hair is pulled back with red and white ribbons. Quico, like the other boys, wears a red kerchief around his neck, a white shirt, and what appear to be blue jeans. Miss Montemayor's version of cowgirls and cowboys; he's even wearing a hat and boots. Walking home from school, in the middle of talk with Anamaría, or with myself—wondering what Chicago was like, a city whose name said two bad words! Or worried about money for whatever crisis was at hand—the afternoon

33

cowboy show creeps into consciousness, and I rush home to find out what's on. We played cowboys and Indians, feeling "Western" for a long time. At the Azteca or the Cine México we watched Pedro Infante or Jorge Negrete be Mexican cowboys who sang and wooed and never fought Indians; and on TV we watched a different story. Those years when we watched Zorro, Hopalong Cassidy, Roy Rogers, The Cisco Kid, The Lone Ranger, we'd imitate movie plots out in the monte behind our house. Every afternoon the black-and-white TV programs would be interrupted by Cowboy Sam, and his sidekick, the blonde wife of the station manager who dressed as a cowgirl in fringed felt and boots, would interview youngsters who wrote and asked to be in the show. I wrote and got admitted to the show; so we went, Dahlia, Tino, and I. Rode the bus downtown and I managed it all without my parents help. "Sí m'ija, but remember you have to take your brother and sister with you," Papi had said when I asked permission. And when they had a story-writing contest, that's when I wrote my very first story—must've been third grade, the memory's fuzzy—every afternoon Tino and I would watch expectantly for the reading of the stories that had been submitted. Cowboy Sam finally read my name and the title of the story, but I was only an honorable mention. I didn't win anything. Not even the reading of the story, not even the case of Coca Cola or the month's supply of frankfurters the ventriloquist advertised with his cowboy dummy. I received the story back with the judges' comments, which I have erased from my memory, but one thing I remember about the story is that it had no female characters and the cowboy, the hero, saved the day for his friend and killed the bad guys in a shoot-out—not very creative and quite predictable given the models in the form of movies and shows I was watching. And all the while, my uncles in Anáhuac herding cattle and being real cowboys, my aunts living out stories no fifties scriptwriter for Mexican movies or U.S. TV ever divined. Peewee, Angelita, Sanjuana, and I, our partners stand behind us, second graders square dancing, counting—

one, two, three, four, under, one two three four, under—as the music blares over the loud speaker.

~ Comadres ~

Tres Mujeres. Vecinas. Comadres. Three women. Neighbors. They pose in front of a frame house, pink with blue trim as if announcing the babies, eight girls and three boys. Three women. They smile and tease each other, look into the camera self-consciously. Tina, the shortest, plump and comfortable with all that weight—it's hereditary, can't do a thing about it! Concha wears a perpetual frown and laughing eyes above ojeras, shadows dark and purple. Mami, does she see herself as the oldest? The most reserved? The one the others come to for advice? She has the most kids, the most talents, from healing a colicky baby to sewing a wedding dress complete with bridesmaids' gowns. The three comadres sharing worries, joys: each morning after the dishes are done, the clothes hung on the line, the beans cooking. Sharing chismes, dreams, gossip, advising each other:

"No, comadre, tell my compadre not to worry. Your compadre will help him put in the cesspool, like ours. Just wait till the summer heat passes, it's not good to do too much during the canícula."

"Sure, come February, you can have some cuttings from my rose-bushes."

"I don't think it matters whether you're married by the church or not, after all, it's not that you didn't want to; you couldn't because compadre Leo was already married by the church, he was divorced. But, you're legally married, so I don't think it matters, you can have your baby baptized, but your compadre will ask Father Jones, just to be sure."

"No, comadre, you already have five boys, what if the next is a boy, too. You're doing the right thing. If your compadre weren't so religious I would've done the same thing, but since he got involved with his Cursillo

35

movement, he won't hear of it. Good thing you found a doctor who would do it, too."

And every morning, platicando, and every evening playing lotería, laughing, chatting, leaning on each other for decisions, for support. Las comadres attend to each other's needs. Early on, it's their own kids running and playing all around, later it's grandchildren who sit on a lap, or need a runny nose wiped, or sleep secure in grandmotherly arms, when they gather to chat in the morning sun. In death, and in birth, there for each other; feeding the kids, doing laundry, sweeping linoleum floors and sunbaked backyards; sometimes pain forming bonds stronger than blood makes them more sisters to each other than to their own sisters, Thelma, Nicha, Tita. Vecinas. Comadres. Above all, women sharing life, tending to each other. Supporting each other. Teaching each other to mother, to survive, to understand, to live. In the picture it's neither the early youthful faces and dark hair, nor the later lined faces and grey-haired women. The three look straight at the camera with laughing eyes, hair blowing in the wind, their solidarity palpable as their love for each other; still to come is the pain of losing a child, of losing a parent, of poverty so acute children go hungry, of illnesses without doctors, of living. In their day, saying "I love you" not allowed, not needed, when their deeds show love every day in many ways for many years. As young wives they flirted with dreams of a wild future, their kids would be lawyers, doctors; fly off and go to better homes, better lives, free of need, of want, free of work— hard and unending—that barely gives enough to stay alive. Aging into comfort and discomfort they celebrate their children's successes: each high school diploma, each college degree, each wedding, each well-paying job, each recognition, each award, each promotion finds them jubilant. They weep for their children's failures, layoffs, divorces, drop-outs, miscarriages, drugs, fights, DWI's, fines, alcoholism, family disturbance calls, moves to far away cities—Chicago, Houston, Dallas,

St. Louis. They share it all, offer sympathy and prayers. Vecinas. Comadres. Mujeres.

∿ *Parade* ∿

In the street in winter, I'm no more than a year old. Papi's walking, holding me. I sit up high above the street in his arms. A street photographer captures us in a crowd. He, lean and thin wearing his good hat and dress clothes, a freshly starched shirt; and I, chubby-cheeked wearing a red, hand-knitted hat and sweater bundled up for winter. So comforting, so secure to be held aloft and feel the security, the strength of his arms. So many times he held me. For some of these there are no photographs. At one point the image of seeing a parade, must've been the George Washington's birthday celebration, for it was downtown and hundreds of soldiers from Mexico and the United States march—drums and trumpets so loud the sound stays in my head; huge military tanks with helmeted soldiers peering from the cubby holes; and little girls from elementary schools from both cities parading, singing, dancing, all in unison; cowboys and Indians on horseback, riding side by side—Pocahontas holding the key to the city—waving and gently guiding the beautiful horses. The floats like giant piñatas, carros alegóricos with young women decked out in shimmering gowns that shine like the sun, escorted by white-wigged young men who stand stiff as statues dressed in satin and lace, and wave mechanically. The flags go by, the men take off their hats, and everyone places a hand over their heart—the same for the U.S. or the Mexican flag, but when the Mexican flag goes by someone in the crowd shouts "¡Viva México!" and everyone answers "¡Viva!" And I atop my Papi's shoulders watching it all go by, freezing images in time, like a camera.

↜ China Poblana One ↝

Smiling I look straight at the camera; I grimace, smile, squint, under bright sun. Must be around noon—not a shadow shows. We have just returned from the George Washington's birthday parade. I hold up my china poblana skirt and point my toe as I stand for the photo. Mami has braided my shoulder-long hair, adding volume and length with yarn— green, white, and red—verde blanco y colorado la bandera del soldado. The dazzlingly white blouse embroidered with bright silk to shape flowers like the ones that grow in our yard—roses, hibiscus, geraniums, and even some that look like the tiny blossoms of the moss roses remind me of summer, although it's a warm February day.

I know Raúl is hiding behind his Dad's car to make fun of me; I pretend not to notice. Instead of his teasing though, I hear a whistle—a wolf whistle—and I become even more upset than if he had called me skinny or wetback, yelled his favorite taunts, *mojada* or *flaca*. I mustn't move because Mami wants me to stand perfectly still until she takes the picture. I resist the urge to grab a stone, hit Raúl with it. My aim is good and I know exactly where he is, if only I could. And I feel like the Chalupa in the lotería game, like María Félix, Dolores del Río, a movie star frozen in costume. But then it's all gone like the dust remolino that came up unexpectedly and left us all dusty. A lonely urraca lets out a loud cawing in the noon heat, predicting a change of weather, warning of the freezing winds that will hit later that afternoon and will cut into my face as I ride the wheel of fortune at the carnival, where I'll bite into pink fluff of sugar and find it disappear into sweetness. We go inside the frame house, have lunch: sopa de arroz, picadillo guisado, and fresh corn tortillas with orange flavored Kool-Aid. Mami tells Bueli that I'm growing so fast the costume won't fit by next year, and Dahlia will wear it to the parade. I cringe and want to cry, but I won't let the thought spoil the present, and I ask if I can buy cotton candy at the carnival. Maybe I'll even win a little pink or blue chick to keep me company. And I do but when the chick becomes a chicken, Bueli wrings its neck, drains the blood, and we have arroz con pollo for Easter.

⌁ *China Poblana Two* ⌁

Mami isn't even nineteen when she's photographed as a china poblana at the plaza in front of Santo Niño de Atocha Church, with a whole setup—fake horse and all. She holds her skirt and points her foot as instructed; on the wide-brimmed charro hat the embroidery screams ¡Viva México! She who wasn't even born in Mexico, who went there as a ten-year-old knowing only to read and write in English because the nuns at Sacred Heart in San Antonio wouldn't tolerate Spanish. Settled in the tiny hamlet of Rodríguez with the sunbaked packed dirt yard, and the two-room adobe; Rodríguez, where school was a few rough-hewn wood benches and a young teacher brimming with socialist ideas—after all it was during the Cárdenas presidency—taught the songs of a nationalism rooted in revolution. She saw her gentleman father drown in self-pity and drink, a gentleman who wrote poems and owned a Model T, a gentleman who took his daughters on picnics to Breckenridge Park and to the beach in Corpus Christi every summer, a gentleman who inherited everything on the Mexican side of the border when his mother died, the maternal family's store in Monclova, Coahuila, and the paternal properties, the ranch in Tamaulipas. He lost everything on both sides because of a curse his own family laid on him—pure jealousy, pura envidia, as the aunts tell it. He sang a favorite song, evenings on the porch in San Antonio, strumming the same guitar he had played when courting Bueli in Monterrey. Bueli's uncles didn't allow her to have anything to do with the foráneo, after all he was from Tejas and who knows who his people were. Of course, Bueli's grandmother couldn't do much—she knew she wouldn't be around to protect the young orphan whose mother had died in childbirth and whose father was always off, a telegrapher for the railroad. In a household of absent men what could she do? And of course Bueli had been flattered and had fallen in love with the handsome romantic Tejano. And she and her grandmother had arranged the "elopement" so that they would be married at her comadre Adela's house both by el civil and by a priest, too. But soon after they were in San Antonio the revolution had come and things were hard. Her uncle had been killed and perhaps her father too. She never knew for sure. Never saw her grandmother again, and many years later visited comadre Adela and her daughters, her childhood friends in Monterrey, couldn't even put flowers on her mother's grave—no one knew where it was. But for her dead children—four she lost when they were barely walking, buried in San Antonio and Corpus Christi, she prays on the day of the angelitos, lights a candle, and makes a mark on the waxy taper and says a prayer for each of their angel souls. Lights another white candle on the day of the dead for her parents and all her adult dead. Teaches me to pray for all the holy souls, las santas ánimas, each night as we set aside a glass of water for the lost souls, las ánimas perdidas.

"When you lose something, just pray thirteen Our Fathers to the ánimas perdidas and you'll find the lost item."

"Can you find lost people, too?" I ask.

"Only if they want to be found," she answers with a twinkle in her honey-colored eyes. And I wonder if she ever tried to find Buelito, when he would disappear for weeks and show up later claiming to have had a job in Zacatecas or in Chicago. Did he want to be found? Mami at sixteen, the breadwinner, posed, one hand holding the horse, the other the sequined skirt so the eagle with the serpent in its beak shows clearly in the photo.

∼ Green Organza ∽

The china poblana is only one of my mother's pictures as a young woman. In another she wears a green evening gown made of the sheerest green organza, looks like gossamer, and the scooped neckline edged in black with her long formal gloves render her a veritable movie star. The young carefree factory worker sews children's dresses during the week, on weekends boards the train loaded with groceries for her mother and her sister; she goes home to Rodríguez and the Sunday plaza promenade, and the trip back early Monday morning. Years later she dances fox trots and danzones and maybe even the boogie-woogie at the VFW with the returning soldiers on her night off from working with the Jewish banker's family; she's the nanny to their first-born daughter. She still travels to Rodríguez on the train and keeps an autograph book where friends write dedicatorias in English and Spanish: "To my dearest friend: Roses are red, violets are blue, remember Manuel, he loves you true." "Del cielo cayó un pañuelo . . ." A carefree teen with family on both sides of a river that's never a barrier; after all, she's Texas-born, her land lies beyond borders.

ᴧ Margarita ᴧ

There is no photo to remind me, but in my mind's eye I see her in the early morning darkness. I've awakened to see Mami keeping vigil, killing mosquitoes with her hands as her children sleep four and five to a bed. I go back to sleep feeling secure, and awaken again to the smell of coffee, to the sound of talk—she and Bueli and Papi in the kitchen. She's rolling out testales the size of tostones, fifty-cent pieces, into thin tortillas my cousin Beto claims are the best in the world. One morning the adult talk is about money, or the lack of it. Mami convincing Papi that without layaways and credit accounts, we'll never have furniture, clothes, the things we need. It's not the way his father did things, on credit. He resists. I sense his frustration, his injured pride. Her common sense wins out. We start signing for groceries—flour, pinto beans, baloney, ground meat—at the tiendita on Saunders. We get the set of encyclopedias, a Sears wringer washing machine. We lay-away clothes for school, for Christmas. But we know not to ask for frivolous things, clothes; we sew, mend. She'll sew, for the neighbors, save what she earns and make do. Things others have, we want, don't dare ask. Eventually, we'll even get a TV set.

At twenty-nine, above the wringer washing machine, Mami laughs as she blows soap bubbles into the air for Margie to chase. Margarita, the first one to be born in a hospital, thanks to Blue Cross. Margie, long auburn hair flying in the wind, wearing nothing but a handmade flour sack print panty—la sirena, Concha calls her, because she loves the water and her hair looks like the mermaid on the lotería card—chasing pretty bubbles, laughing under the hot morning sun, running barefoot, "Más, Mami, más," she cries. And Mami lifts a handful of foam and blows more bubbles into the air. Mami's life shaped by laughter and tears: crying till the tears ran out when Tino was killed, when Margie was divorced, when

43

I first left, and suffering all of our misfortunes; when you give life to eleven children and suffer two miscarriages you don't take worrying or life lightly. Every day brings its weight of worries and of joys, laughter and tears like sunshine and rain.

↶ *Blue Stroller* ↷

I'm in the stroller that I suspect came with us from the other Laredo. A young Bueli is pushing it, dressed in her late-forties platform shoes and tailored dress, her hair up in a chignon. My memory for everything but the stroller is like the photo, black and white; the stroller is the blue of my winter coat when I was sixteen. When I saw the coat on the rack at J. C. Penney's, I had to have it. Spent almost all I'd earned proofreading for the weekly community paper on that coat. Years later I realized it reminded me of that stroller. Painted blue, made of metal and wood. I remember it well; we used it until Margie was born. Just like my periquera—the fancy high chair that could be converted into a toy wagon, and the crib that rocked like a cradle that Papi repainted and redecorated with bunnies, cubs, kittens, and other baby animal decals for each birth; things were used and reused. Children's furniture and other pieces, too, as when Papi's old desk became our desk. It held his old books and magazines, correspondence courses: electrician, magician, even auto mechanic. Dreams of what he'd wanted to be. And some adult joke books that were hidden away from prying eyes—mine. He emptied it of his things, painted it red for Tino's school things. In the photo I'm an infant—chubby, puffy cheeks, and under a hat, little hair—oblivious to what is going on, more interested in playing with a rattle, with the red, yellow, green, and blue wooden balls strung on a wire. Mami, a young woman takes the photo, nineteen when I was born; does she see herself ten years and five children later? Twenty years from then, ten children later?

⌁ Lola's Wedding ⌁

It's a wedding—the photo taken as we stand on the front steps of Sagrado Corazón Church in Monterrey. Papi's family's all there—Lola's marrying Pepe! At Tía Chacha's I've seen the portrait the groom painted of my cousin—it's too flattering; "love is blind" and "must be love" everyone says, but I think Lola beautiful with her alabaster skin, just like the Virgin Mary's statue, her color-of-amber hair and her laughing grey eyes. I'm impressed, is he a famous artist? Will they be in love forever? Tati, her youngest sister, is flower girl along with Pepe's youngest sister. Tati's only a month younger than I, but because she's in the wedding party is acting older. It's winter and the bridesmaids and the flower girls wear dark pink velvet dresses. My parents are padrinos de cojines, and walk in

47

carrying the cushions where the bride and groom will kneel. The photographer catches them walking out. Mami's dress is also velvet, black—soft as a kitten's fur; the rose satin bodice under black cotton lace is movie-star elegant. And although in 1957 hats aren't much bigger than a diadem, Mami's put fine black net on hers, crowns her hair permed for the occasion. Papi has on a new suit and his aftershave lingers as they pass down the aisle. The photographer captures their solemn faces. None of my siblings have come; I act grown up, but Tía Chacha insists I sit at the children's tables at the reception in the big elegant hall with the red carpet and the marble dance floor. Thirty years later, when Pepe died, a distraught Lola came to visit me in Madrid, to forget her pain—cried her eyes out listening to Rocío Durcal sing "Amor Eterno" at the open-air concert. She spent hours remembering the ups and downs, the moves to Chicago—the Panadería Nuevo León in the heart of Pilsen, with the best pan dulce in Chicago—back to Monterrey and the restaurant business; to Sabinas—the restaurant by the ojo de agua—to Monterrey again, and at last to Laredo and the truck stop with the best chicken-fried steak in South Texas—Pepe always the entrepreneur, always into "business," always in love with her, of that she was sure.

"Nos quisimos tanto," she would begin each story and break into tears. Most of the children grown and married, her youngest only twelve and needing a father. At sixty, she's come back to her mother's home—works part time, plays bingo at the hall by IH 35 with the giant Border Bingo sign—she's come home, a home unlike the one she left in Monterrey to go to Sagrado Corazón Church where her father walked her down the aisle. The house of her youth had marble floors and big windows and walls covered with expensive flossed wallpaper; this one has cement floors covered with linoleum and thin sheetrock walls painted pastel pink; dust covers everything—the knick-knacks her grandchildren have given her, the toothpick holder that says Epcot Center, the tiny bell with

"Six Flags," and the garish green ceramic ashtray little Pepito has made for her in school that proclaims "I ♡ grandma."

In the sweltering South Texas afternoons the whirring of the air-conditioning lulls her to sleep; each night she dreams of trips to Las Vegas, of Pepe and dances at the exclusive Cueva Leonística in Monterrey, the months of courtship, when she posed for her portrait, her mother furious with her because of her rebellions, her father understanding and tolerant of his wild daughter with the heart of gold.

⤙ Mase ⤚

Maximiano. To many, plain Max; to us, Tío Mase, Mami's cousin, Tino's first communion padrino. In the photo they stand at the church door; San Luis Rey is in full crusader's armor in bas relief above them. Mase in a dark suit, his hand on Tino's shoulder. Tino dressed in white holding the candle, the missal, the rosary, smiling at the camera. In the formal photo at the studio, Tino's smile mirrors Mase's smile, proof to Mami that Tino takes after her side of the family, after her father. At Tino's funeral, Mase solemnly walks up to Mami and Papi. They'd already grieved at home in that time between, when we all waited and wept, but here it's public. Only a few can see the tears escape as he kneels before the vacuum-sealed coffin, pray before the ahijado he loved as a son. In the photo a much younger Mase than I ever knew. Mami and Mase, sit on a green wrought-iron bench in the plaza in Nuevo Laredo. They relish the opportunity to sit, talk, laugh as the street photographer jokes with them, thinking them sweethearts. Their sisters Nicha and Lupe have walked away, not wanting to be photographed. A few months later, Mase goes to the front. The family worries, prays, hopes. Tía Chole prays the rosary for his safe return, goes to 6:00 A.M. Mass at El Divino Redentor, a daily ritual that works, for he returns and she hangs his picture and his medals on her living room wall in the tiny, two-room house on Guadalupe Street. When she died everything stayed the same. Her sisters Nana and Choco moved in. Now they have even buried Tío Mase. Nothing goes according to plan. When Tía Chole adopted her cousin's son, the daughter—Lupe—went to another aunt; she fought her sisters Nana and Choco. She was the only one married at the time and couldn't see how they could even pretend to care for an infant. Mase became the center of her world. She often led strangers to believe he was her own, born of her own body. But Nana and Choco never let her forget that she was an usurper. With the GI Bill Mase studied, set up his printing business, and married Lucía, his high school sweetheart, and had eight children—seven daughters and Junior, the youngest. Many a Saturday evening at their house, after carne asada dinners, we would eat homemade popsicles, frozen ice cubes of cinnamon tea with milk. While Mami, Tía Lucía, and Bueli visited and Mase and Papi watched wrestling on TV, we played "a la touch," or "la roña," or "retratos." We played "bebeleche" when we could draw the hopscotch diagram on the ground, and "a las escondidas," hiding under the house in the darkening evening, scared of spiders and scorpions and most of all of Tía Lucía who would lash out at anyone who transgressed in any number of ways. Her own daughters, the target of most of her punishments, sought refuge in their Dad's understanding and forgiving heart.

High school graduation announcements, wedding invitations, and photos carefully put away amongst his things in the shop. He had retired and only occasionally took on printing jobs—usually wedding invitations or birth announcements for family. His fingers perpetually darkened by the ink of his trade. I loved to snoop in the little shop behind the house: the smell of ink, of paper, of freshly printed words, black as fate on the eggshell white of wedding announcements. My image of him when Mami,

Papi, and I went to ask that he print my quinceañera invitations: sweat runs down his forehead, down his bare arms; he wore an undershirt and brown pants, the leather belt darkened by the sweat. The fan in the corner of his shop, just moving the hot air around, only pretending to offer surcease from the oppressive heat of that afternoon.

Almost thirty years later it's a May evening when I see him in his final resting place, looks serene. I give my pésame to the family, hugging the ones I know, Lucy, Fela, Sara, and shaking hands with the younger ones I don't know. The youngest daughters don't recall our visits, instead remember coming to visit us at our house on San Carlos Street on Sunday afternoons and playing with my younger siblings. But, Lucy, Fela, and Sara remembered. Tía Lucia with her dyed, jet black hair, sits between her mother and her daughters, surrounded by grandchildren and her sister-in-law, Lupe, back from Chicago with her husband, with stories of when they were young, comparing their memory of me as a child of eight—their own son only a few months younger than I, now married and settled with four children and three grandchildren in Chicago. Of course, las Tías—Nana and Choco, in their nineties, still living in the old house where walls are full of photographs, remembering the young Mase in high school, in his soldier's uniform, remembering Buelito and the songs he played on his guitar. Mase's sons-in-law hover around the daughters. Lucy's Anglo husband, her son a strange mixture of her husband's Irish features and her father's mestizo coloring, that certain look in the eye. The others, Juan, Luis, Ovidio, mourn a father.

When I see the blurred photo of a smiling Tío Mase in the obituary section of the *Laredo Morning Times*, I hear his throaty laugh, his mango sweet voice, "Es Todo" and "Way to Go" forever encouraging and forever proud of us all. His legacy for his daughters and for a distant niece: his laughter, his comfort, his solid support. I can still taste the milky cinnamon ice cubes, heladitos, melting in my thirsty mouth between games of

51

bebeleche and hide-and-go-seek and his voice mixing Spanish and English so unlike Papi's Spanish-only voice, greeting Papi, "Quihúbole, Primo," his love for Mami, clear in his despedida, ""See you later, Prima, cuídese."

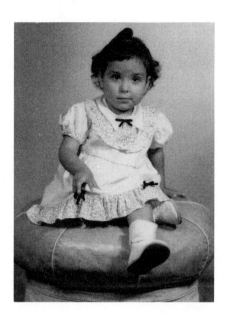

↵ *Nena at Three* ↳

The three-year-old girl looks off camera, probably at her father who dangles a pair to keys to make her laugh, or at least smile. She does and the photographer snaps the photo, freezes the image of the little girl wearing the yellow dress, yellow ribbon, tiny gold loops on her earlobes, a gold chain on her fat wrist. The yellow dress, a black velvet ribbon bow at the neckline, short puffy sleeves, a wide ruffled skirt covers the pudgy legs. Wearing white leather boots she sits on an ottoman-like throne, her hand rests on her knee, feels the soft yellow cotton piqué; she smiles with her whole body.

Her mother brushed and combed and neatly side-parted the curls, one curl pinned up crowns her above uneven bangs. The studio is quiet except for the voices, her mother's soft cooing and her father's teasing voice; they call her name and ask her to smile, "Nena, ríete, ríete, mira; Nena, mira para acá . . ." They stand by the black box with legs. The photographer's hidden under a black cloth; suddenly after the flash like nothing she's ever seen, he comes out, just like that, out of nowhere, smiling. The black walls, the bright lights, the flash frightens her, makes her cry. From that smile she wears on the picture, she goes to the screams of fear and sobbing as her father takes her in his arms "ya ya, ya no llores, ya pasó."

"A la edad de tres años," reads the inscription on the photo framed in black that Tía Nicha keeps on her repisita in the corner of her living room.

Mami keeps another one in the shoe box, and there's one in an album Esperanza put together one summer. This photograph stays with me— I'm only three and it must be important—I was a happy child; I recall wearing the yellow dress to Mass, trying to undo the tiny black velvet ribbon bows decorating the skirt. I'm as happy as when riding the ponies at the carnival or eating a pirulí, the happiness of innocence—feeling valued, loved. My eyes are sad though. As if I were thinking of the pain, the loss, the burdens that are to come. Funny how some sadness seeps onto the look, la mirada, even on my three-year-old face. The feelings of future loneliness creeps in—oh, what a strange look for a three-year-old. Does one know what is to come, even at three? All those brothers and sisters, all the work and the worry. What will happen to the photo once I'm gone, who will remember the sad child? No child will think fondly of it as its mother's photo. The photo, a montage of one cool January day when I was three.

⤳ Last Piñata ⤲

We're in our backyard for my last birthday piñata. In the foreground the piñata in the shape of a birthday cake, a clothesline directly in front of the camera. Neighbors, cousins, siblings. In the background, in the half-finished kitchen my father was adding to our four-room frame house, sit the adults: Doña Carmen, Concha, Romana, Tina, Tía Nicha, others. I'm in the middle, curly hair rising like a headpiece. Thin legs end in white socks and black patent-leather shoes. Esperanza is only three and she's ambling away from the group, as if not interested, or more interested in something outside of the photograph. I've lost the photo, I don't even know where it is, in one of my Mother's other boxes, or in one of Espy's albums, perhaps. It remains crisp and clear in my mind. I recall the dress I am wearing: a blue plaid with white and red interlocking stripes, a white cotton piqué collar. It's store bought, not handmade by Mami who had bought it from Doña Carmen, who'd bring ready-made dresses from the stores downtown and resell for outrageous prices. The utter joy of the day lives in color, although the fuzzy, out-of-focus photo is black and white. A Sunday afternoon. Mami's gone all out for me and for Esperanza—the party strategically timed between both our birthdays. I can't explain the feelings I get or why I remember the photo so clearly. Perhaps my getting older, knowing it was my last piñata. I cried over the birthday cake as I put out the candles, not even my quinceañera compares with it. But that's another story, and another photo—taken in our front yard.

⤙ *Communions* ⤚

It's my first first communion; in two weeks I'll take my second first communion. Papi thought it funny, but only after he scolded me for getting the dates mixed up and making Tía Luz come to be my godmother two weeks early. She brought the usual Monterrey goodies—leche quemada, quesos, semitas de Bustamante, and of course, some fresh corn tortillas—along with the first communion requirements: a candle, long and beautiful ecru wax with pink flowers and pale green leaves wrapped around the bottom; a missal with the picture of a blonde child receiving communion from a long-haired, red-robed Jesus on the cover. Most of the text was in Spanish, prayers and such, but the Mass was in Latin—red for what the priest would say, black for what the monaguillos would reply. The next year, when Tino becomes an altar boy, I too memorize the Credo and the Pater Noster and the Gloria in Excelsis in Latin along with all the other replies. My first first holy communion. The scolding and all the preparations lessened my fear of going to confession and receiving Jesus—a concept that I never did understand so I confessed to the same sins over and over for years—I hit my brother and sisters, I disobeyed Mami, I told a lie, I didn't say my prayers. I walked down the aisle alone in Mami's creation, a long organdy gown and a veil held by a diadem, the corona with tiny orange blossoms, just like a bride, Bueli said. Later at Serrano Studio, I smile looking off camera, kneeling and holding the candle, the rosary and the missal just so, a part of Serrano's holy communion setup. "Es fotogénica," Tía Luz exclaims, and I learn a new word.

Two weeks later I walk in with my regular catechism class led by Sister Consuelo to make my first holy communion again. Father Jones winks as he catches my eye. I close my eyes right before he places the paper-tasting wafer on my tongue. Tía Nicha stands by me, my madrina for my second first holy communion. That Sunday morning in May, we came home to chocolate and cake as if it were truly the first time I had received Jesus. Twenty years later when I attended funky Masses where we ate herb bread I had baked and drank wine Bill had made I would flashback and try to count how many first holy communions I had had.

⨍ Panchita ⨎

Panchita came around weekly with her bags full of "encargos" and to collect money owed on merchandise bought on time. She was our Avon Lady; instead of the "ding-dong" of the doorbell, we heard "Ave Maria Purísima," and Mami or Bueli or whoever was closest would answer, "Sin pecado concebida." She also sold Stanley products, clothing, and odds and ends, to be paid at a dollar a week. Instead of cash she would also accept Gold Star or S&H Green stamp books—but only full ones, which she would then exchange for lamps, wall sconces, cookware, and other miscellaneous necessities and trinkets, which she would then sell to her clientes. In the photo, she sits amid a group of preschoolers at her escuelita where she taught the alphabets—English and Spanish—numbers, colors, and rhymes. The same things she had learned as a child attending one of the earliest escuelitas in the twenties. She had learned to read and write in Spanish and became a teacher in a tradition that all but disappeared when Head Start came. From my second-grade classroom I could see her young charges playing in her front yard; she fed them cookies she baked and tepid Kool-Aid. Once, one of her students, my four-year-old sister Dahlia, angry about something, "escaped" during nap time and was about to cross the major highway on her way home; from my classroom, I saw her; I ran to stop her and took her back crying and kicking to Panchita's escuelita. My teacher, Mrs. Treviño, didn't stop me or say a word when I returned to my desk, all upset and hot from the running and struggling with my sister.

Panchita had been widowed; she raised four kids on her own with her sales and her escuelita in the barrio Las Cruces across the street from Saunders School and only two blocks from San Luis Rey Church. Paco, her oldest son, would bring home F's and tell her it meant he was doing "Fine." She wasn't fooled, but didn't have the energy to fight so she would tell the story and laugh. Some twenty years later she changed religions, called everyone "Hermana" and "Hermano"—she had become an "aleluya" so that Paco would change his ways, stop drinking and beating his wife and kids. She would read the Bible whenever she could; Mami finally told her that she didn't believe in reading the Bible but in living it. Panchita stayed away. Years later, when I attended daily Mass for my brother's safe return from 'Nam, I thought I spied her in a back pew at San Luis Rey Church. But, although she acknowledged my greeting, she didn't seem to recognize me.

Panchita, the Avon Lady, smiles from the photo, her daughter Irma stands to her right, Paco sits cross-legged at her feet. She sits, hands crossed on her lap, her students surround her. Dahlia stands to her right, a foot turned inward and her hands at her waist. Defiant.

⁓ *Body Hair* ⁓

An awkward teen, shy and reticent, I face the camera, wearing a sleeveless, morning-glory-blue cotton blouse. My eighth-grade school picture—not many others exist from that time when I suffered the pains of growing up—literally leg cramps that kept me up all night and which Mami would rub with "volcánico," a foul-smelling ointment for horses, and the more subtle but just as painful growing pains, for which there was no salve, of being thirteen and the victim of so many changes. During lunch time, I'm reading in the cafeteria. Nearby, Sarah, the daughter of the Jewish family Mami worked for before she married, is talking to Susan and Janice in a voice loud and clear so I can hear, "All I know is unplucked brows and hairy legs and underarms make a girl look like a boy." The tears streaming down my hot face I run to the bathroom where some of the chucas are smoking. I blurt it out, what they said; they've been after me to pluck my brows, shave my legs. We talk about them as if they were from another planet. "No les hagas caso a esas pendejas," says Rita, who came back last year from El Norte, wearing makeup and talking dirty. Her thick braid held with a red rubber band is all I see as I sniffle and control my tears. I feel torn; these same "pendejas" are sometimes my friends and we work on school projects together; I go to their ritzy houses in the Heights amazed that their parents aren't around, that they drive cars, that they go across to Nuevo Laredo, that they drink and smoke. I'm torn but I believe Rita; they don't know what they're talking about—Mami doesn't shave or pluck her eyebrows either, neither did her comadres until much later. Many Chicana classmates behave like gringas, but my friends, most of us who ride the Saunders bus, we don't yet shave, much less pluck our eyebrows, or wear makeup—our parents forbid it. The bell rings and as I walk back to English class to our Friday quiz, head held high like the protagonist in the book I'm reading, *Head High, Ellen Brodie*, I whisper to Rosario, the only other Chicana in the accelerated class, "I bet we can beat them." I can tell she smiles even though I can't see her face: her ears with the Mexican gold loops redden, and she silently nods "Let's." And we both know who I mean, and we do. But it is Susan's paper that Mrs. McDonnell reads from on Monday morning as an example of good work.

Two years later, it's the same group. And it's jeweled pumps and penny loafers. I beg and beg Mami for a pair of black leather flats with red, green, yellow, shiny rhinestones just like Lydia's. When I finally get them, Papi wants us to take them back—they're shoes for a puta, not a decent girl. But Mami's on my side, after all we spent her hard-earned money on the shoes, so I keep the shoes but wear them rarely. To church and school I wear my old scuffed oxblood red loafers and bobby sox. I'm wearing the rhinestone flats defiantly in my quinceañera photo as I sit in our front yard with friends and family all around.

～ Declamación ～

Declamación—as a three-year-old I stand up on a stage at Mother Cabrini Church looking out at the audience, our neighbors, the priest, the
nuns; Papi is the master of ceremonies, and I recite Mother's Day poems
I learn at Sra. Piña's escuelita: "Si vieras mamita . . ." and "Un día por la
mañana . . ." Later in eighth grade English class I stand to recite "Invic-
tus," which Mrs. McDonell made us all memorize, and it's a "declamación" I do. "No, no, no," her voice stops me, when I've barely begun,
"Dark as the pit from pole to pole," gesturing to the depths and with a
voice forceful and ominous. "This is a reading, not a dramatic perfor-
mance." I start again, attempting to imitate the bland (in my opinion)
reading that Louise had just done. But the words are gone without the
ademanes, the gestures served a mimetic function—the words without
the hand, eye, head movements keep getting tripped in my mind. Like
with the spelling of *John*—I could never get the *h* in the right place: if it
was *ghost* why not *Jhon* I asked? It was no use. I had to sit down and try
again the next day. Cost me 10 points—not being prepared for a reading
when I was scheduled, but the humiliation was worse than getting a 90
instead of a 100.

Then at home, declamando for New Year's and for parties. Tino and I
testing our memorization skills, competing to see who could declamar
the longest poems and remember the most lyrics from songs—in English
and Spanish: "El brindis del bohemio," "The Raven," "Porque me dejé del
vicio," "Anabelle Lee," "El Seminarista de los ojos negros," and on and on
through high school when we would write down the lyrics to our favorite
songs: "La cama de piedra," "México lindo y querido," "Sad Movies Make
Me Cry," "Go Away Little Girl," "Angelito." We start listening to mostly
English: Righteous Brothers, Andy Williams, the Platters, groups like the
Stones and the Beatles. Some Mexican groups and singers: Alberto Vás-
quez, Carlos Guzmán, Sunny and the Sunliners. We forget our declama-

ción and our contests—too childish, too cursi, too Spanish. I often wonder if he thought about those poems when he wrote poetry in 'Nam. When I listen to a niece or a nephew declamar for a school contest I cheer in my heart to hear the spirited words, watch their gestures, and I feel my throat catch a sigh. Although my brother and I were good, no one could surpass Cousin Magda who studied in Bellas Artes and now holds workshops for teachers who want to train their students in the art of "declamación."

∽ Doña Carmen ∼

Doña Carmen and Don Vicent Baca lived across from us on San Carlos Street and didn't have children: she, dark and tall, three times the size of Mami; he, blonde and petite, half the size of Papi. He worked downtown at Salinas Fine Fashions until he retired with a pension, and she stayed home, sold children's clothes, cortes—three-yard cuts of material—that Mami would sometimes buy on time to make our dresses for Easter, Christmas, or our back-to-school clothes: dresses, skirts, blouses for the girls; shirts, pants, and jackets for my brother and my cousin. Doña Carmen held the best posadas at Christmas time. Mami was the madrina one year; she sewed the most beautiful outfit for the baby Jesus—of white tulle, embroidered in white silk, complete with knitted cap and socks— we all helped with the preparativos, although we usually did anyway, even when it was some other neighbor who was the madrina. From the tamalada on Christmas Eve, for the acostar al niño, the singing of Mexican carols, and later because we kids insisted, English ones as well, the champurrado and the little bags of goodies (oranges, pecans, Mexican cookies), and the colaciones and other Christmas candy that fell from the star-shaped piñata that invariably Toño, the oldest of the neighborhood bullies, would break, Doña Carmen's posada was the best. On the sixth of January she prepared a Rosca with a tiny ceramic baby baked right in it, and although the custom was that whoever got the baby would host the Levantar al Niño on February 2, Doña Carmen always hosted the party, although not as elaborate as the Christmas Eve posada. Mami always told us to offer prayers of thanksgiving, and as I followed the others at the conclusion of the Acostar and of the Levantar al Niño when we each came up and kissed Baby Jesus, I thanked Doña Carmen.

✒ Polka Dots ✒

Doña Carmen gives me a polka-dotted corte for my birthday, the jelly-bean colors dancing on white piqué. Mami picks a pattern from a dress in the Sears catalogue. In the photo, Dahlia, Esperanza, and I wear matching Easter dresses Mami's trimmed at the neck and hem lined with three rows of red, blue, green rick-rack, a different color for each of us. In that black-and-white photo, we hold Easter baskets full of jelly beans, marshmallow eggs, and cascarones bright as the confetti they're stuffed with. We've eaten the marshmallow chicks, yellow as egg yolks, so sweet they hurt even Tía Nicha's teeth, and we get her a glass of water. In our matching frocks, our smiles belie future wars, fights for our selves, our growing up pains: Dahlia's biting, her convulsions brought about by worms; Esperanza's furious fights with Dahlia all through high school; my insufferable older-sister syndrome. Three sisters vying for identities as varied as our hair—Dahlia's straight, sun-bleached, honey-colored corn-silk; Espy's black-as-coal thick curls, and my wispy, thin, dark brown wavy locks.

✒ Don Vicente ✒

On Saturday mornings, Don Vicente would recruit the boys to help him clean the yard, pile up dead leaves and branches from the fruit trees—peach, pomegranate, plum-trees whose fruit Doña Carmen generously shared with her neighbors. Her peach preserves on fresh flour tortillas were one of my favorite after-school snacks. Once they swept the trash and other debris into manageable-sized piles, they stood around the bonfires the size of the outdoor oven where he cooked cabecitas de cabrito. After the boys would sweat and play working along side of him, he would pay them a quarter each. Most of the younger boys were grateful for even that, but some argued with him; Gera and Junior, furious because they got exactly the same as the younger huerquillos, boycotted the Saturday morning job until he agreed to pay them fifty cents for their work. But Dahlia was jealous of the boys' jobs; why not hire the girls, too? She fought and argued with Don Vicente. Even fought with the boys, threw rocks at the Lópezes' house till José came out and scolded her. She got her way. Soon she too was working on the Baca's yard, getting paid just like the boys.

⌁ A Baby ⌁

After many prayers, a child, an infant but a few days old, came into their lives. They registered her as their own daughter, the birth mother sent back to Mexico with money and the assurance that her daughter had found a home. But only six months later, when none of the home remedies for fever worked, Mami and Doña Carmen rushed the child to the hospital. She died that night, like a candle that burned herself up; and the light left Doña Carmen's eyes. She blamed herself for being deaf and not hearing the child's cries, for not knowing how to mother, for trusting God. She was broken, lost so much weight that her clothes and her skin hung from her bones like sackcloth. She was shrinking before our very eyes. Depressed and alienated she didn't want anything to do with anyone, fought with the neighbors, with Don Vicente, even with Mami, her comadre. When Papi brought Father Jones to talk with her she ran him off, wouldn't go back to church; God had let her down.

When Doña Carmen buried Don Vicente we knew she wouldn't last long. In spite of her bragging that she never needed anyone, in spite of her fights, everyone looked out for her. One day after school, an ambulance, huge and white like a ship in our school history books, came to swallow her into the white vastness; we barely stopped our taunts and shouting, "que llueva, que llueva, la virgen de la cueva" at the ominous clouds that darkened the five-o'clock sky. She never came back. Her nephew came from San Antonio, held the velorio at a funeral home, so many of the neighbors didn't attend the rosary or the wake. Even before we had finished praying her novena, he emptied the house, piled everything in the backyard, and set a match to it. The fire even burned some of the trees; he sold the lot, the abandoned house and all in it to a developer who tore the house down, sending mice and rats and all kinds of animals looking for new homes. In the photo Doña Carmen's eyes look through glasses thick as time, she wears her homemade dress with the pocket for her hearing aid, and her hand big as a loaf of bread rests on Don Vicente's thin shoulder.

⌁ Martha's Mamagrande ⌁

Los Valdezes kept their grandmother in a cuartito in their backyard. She was agonizing, en agonía, they said. She spoke to the angels and sang holy songs all night and didn't let anyone, especially not her son, Antonio, sleep. But even when they emptied out the small shed in the back and she was moved there, the son couldn't sleep thinking of his mother out there, alone, singing and talking to the angels. But at least the children slept. The lack of sleep was getting to him; he would fall asleep at work. Papi would come home and tell Mami how he and the other men covered for Toño so "El Viejo" wouldn't fire him from his laborer job at the antimony smelter that laid them off twice a year like clockwork—at Christmas and in the summer. I was curious and wanted to ask what the angels looked like and what they said. Toño, Martha's older brother, laughed at me and said, "You're as crazy as Mamagrande." Martha said her father didn't want anyone talking to her Mamagrande. As to the angels, it was a lie.

"No es cierto." Martha, older than I, spoke with authority, "Mamagrande's just crazy, everyone knows angels don't appear to old people."

"Why not?" I asked.

"No se, but they don't. A ver, in Fátima, at Lourdes, it's always children, and besides that was the Virgin who appeared to them."

"But what about the Virgin Mary," I asked, not quite following Martha's argument.

"What about her?" Martha asked, exasperated, wanting to get back to our game of bebeleche.

"Well, the Angel Gabriel appeared to her," I argued feebly.

"She was a child, too, she was only fifteen, Mamagrande's almost a hundred."

One afternoon we were playing comadritas in Martha's yard, I'm chewing a mesquite bean pod. I sneaked to the backyard pretending to look for pebbles that look like peas for our pretend sopa de arroz. As I approached the cuartito, I heard Martha's Mamagrande softly singing a lullaby; her voice so soft it was more like a murmur, and I had to strain to hear the words: "Señora Santa Ana; porqué llora el niño? Por una manzana que se le ha perdido . . ." It was the same song Bueli sang when she rocked Espy to sleep. And then I heard a voice, louder and much clearer, coming through the boards of the shack, singing "Oh María, Madre Mía, Oh Consuelo del mortal, ampararnos y guiarnos a la puerta celestial." Martha's Mamagrande joined the other voice and both continued the song which I knew so well. I almost joined in the familiar tune. Suddenly frightened, I realized what was happening, rushed to where Dahlia, Carmela, and Martha were pretending to cook mole with a thick reddish mud paste. I dropped the pebbles in the make-believe sopa and went

67

home and looked for Bueli, gave her a big hug, my arms around her waist. Her apron smelled of onions. When I started crying, she held me and asked me what was wrong, I couldn't talk. Martha's Mamagrande died the next day. At the wake, Martha's father cried like a baby in front of the coffin. When it was my turn, I didn't want to kneel and pray in front of the coffin; Papi ordered me to, so I did. When I saw her wrinkled face, I thought someone had taken ashes from the fire and used it for powder, I started to cry and I reached out and touched her equally ashen hand—there was not a trace of ashes. She held a black rosary. A picture of a Guardian Angel protecting two blonde children as they walk on a bridge that's about to collapse was pinned to the casket.

"That's the color of death," Martha informed me later when I asked if they had indeed covered her Mamagrande with ashes.

The adults all wore black and we couldn't watch television, not even listen to the radio soaps or Serenata Nocturna or anything for nine whole days. Every evening right after sunset, we gathered at the Valdezes and knelt, squeezed in their living room where the coffin had been. And we prayed the rosary every night, the mirrors remained covered, the candles lit for those nine days. As we walked back to our own home, Bueli would cross herself and point to a tall cubreviento; but no matter how much I tried, I couldn't see the owl she claimed was there watching us. Sometimes, though, I thought I heard the song the angels sang over and over in my mind.

⤳ Halloween ⤵

It's Halloween, but we haven't donned costumes—we didn't yet believe in that strange U.S. custom; only my younger siblings did many years later. Mamagrande and her oldest daughter, Tía Lydia, have come to visit, to clean the lápida in Nuevo Laredo where Mamagrande's dead children are buried, to place fresh flowers in tin cans wrapped in foil, and hang beautiful wreaths; they've come to honor the dead. But it's the day before, and Mami and Papi and Bueli leave me alone with our guests and the kids; I'm fixing dinner—showing off that I can cook and feed the kids. I've made the flour tortillas, measuring ingredients with my hands, the way Mami and Bueli do, five handfuls of flour, some salt, a handful of shortening, some espauda from the red can marked "KC." Once it's all mixed in, the shortening broken into bits no bigger than peas, I pour hot water, almost boiling but not quite, and knead the dough, shape it into a fat ball like a bowl turned over. I let it set while I prepare the sauce I will use for the fideo. When it's time, I form the small testales the size of my small fist; I roll out the tortillas, small and round, the size of saucers, and cook them on the comal. As they cook, I pile them up on a dinner plate, wrap them in a cloth embroidered with a garland of tiny flowers—red, blue, yellow—and crochet-edged in pale pink. We eat fideo, beans, tortillas quietly because Mamagrande and Tía Lydia watch us. We drink the cinnamon tea with milk. I look outside and see a huge moon rising; it's the same color as the warm liquid in my cup. Later, Tino and Dahlia wash the dishes, and even later, the kids are watching TV quietly, without arguing. Mamagrande rocks in the sillón out on the porch and can't understand why some kids all ragged and costumed as hoboes and clowns come and ask for treats. I try to explain, but it's useless. My siblings want "fritos" so I cut some corn tortillas Mamagrande has brought from Monterrey into strips and heat the grease in an old skillet. I'm busily frying the strips and soaking the grease off on a clean dishrag when all of a sudden the skillet turns and I see the hot grease fall as if in slow motion. My reflexes are good, but the burning on my foot tells me I wasn't fast enough. At first it doesn't hurt, but then I feel it—the skin and to the bone, as if a million cactus thorns—the tiny nopal thorns—have penetrated my foot, I scream with pain. Mamagrande rushes and puts butter

69

on the burn. I cry. The kids are scared. Later, Doña Lupe will have to do healings de susto—they're so frightened. And when Mami and Papi return they scold me for not being careful.

I miss school for two days. When I go back, my foot and ankle wrapped in gauze and cotton bandages attract attention. I'm embarrassed. When my social studies teacher, Mrs. Kazen, the wife of a future senator, concerned, asks, I tell her the truth.

"Did you go to the hospital? Did a doctor examine the burn?"

"No," I answer, knowing it's the wrong answer, but not wanting to lie.

She shakes her head, so I know not to tell her how every three hours, day and night for three days, Mami, remembering Bueli's remedios, has been putting herb poultices on the burn and cleaning it thoroughly. She's punctured the water-filled ámpula with a maguey thorn and tells me there won't even be a scar. And there isn't.

⌁ Camposanto ⌁

Mamagrande returned to Monterrey perplexed by the children who had come to our door shyly asking "trick or treat?" and fleeing when she told them to go away. I remembered Bueli and missed lighting candles for the ánimas perdidas. We had prayed so her dead would find peace. But what I regretted most was missing the visit to the camposanto to visit Buelito's tomb, because you couldn't visit if you were sick or had a wound, even something as minor as a scratch, much less a burn like mine. So I stayed across the street at Mami's friend's house where the daughters Alicia and Adela sat amidst stacks of paper—foil, tissue, crepe—and busily fixed flower arrangements and put finishing touches on wreaths of marigold-yellow, sky-blue, and bougainvillea-purple crepe paper flowers. Roses, red, white, salmon, yellow, my favorites, they make them in all stages—from barely budding ones to those in full bloom with petals that turn and twist, bloom just like real roses. Their father, Don Viviano cuts sugarcane stalks that lean against the wall, tall as the house, into foot-long pieces. He hacks the stalks with a machete the size of a sword. Chewing the cane for the juicy caña syrup, I turn to the book I've brought. Don Viviano tells me how his son Raúl so loved to read, he went crazy. "Everyone knows that's what books do to you. Yes, Raúl had a strong head, a strong mind, but he still succumbed and became like a child. Of course, it could've been a curse one of his girlfriends put on him, when he wouldn't marry her and preferred his books to her. In any case, it's the books," Don Viviano tells me "that's what weakens the head, the mind, makes one turn crazy." I stop reading and think of Raúl, I barely remember him: a silent young man, reddish hair and green eyes, sitting on a stool in the corner of the tiny kitchen.

"What happened to Raúl?" I ask.

"May he be at peace," Don Viviano says solemnly and gestures with his head toward the camposanto. I want to ask more, but he gets up, sullen, and silently walks into the house. I think of the camposanto.

ᴧ Huesario ᴧ

From Don Viviano's front yard where I sit, beyond the low wall, I can see the huesario. I'd never noticed it until the year before. I'd been afraid Buelito's bones might end up there. Mami had reassured me, no, only those who don't own their own terreno are disinterred, their bones thrown into the huesario; she and Tía Nicha had paid for Buelito's terreno, so I had nothing to fear. They had also planted the maguey at his feet like he had always said he wanted—he loved tequila that much! His was a poor tomb with only a simple cross that read "Maurilio Ramón," the dates faded and undecipherable—quite a poor tomb compared to the one that housed Mamagrande's dead, that monument spanned two lots and was made of heavy marble; so far it housed five of her seven

71

dead children: Lucita, who had been killed at twelve by a stray bullet when she was walking to the corner store with her friend; Anita, who had died of a fever at age two; Gonzalo, who had been stabbed in a fight at a dance and died instantly (he was thirty-two); and the two "angelitos" who had died only hours after birth—twins she had named Rafael and Refugio after her brothers. The other two were buried in the Las Minas cemetery in Dolores upriver from Laredo; no one ever visited them; they'd died in infancy when the family lived there between the time of the Revolution and the First World War. I regretted not being able to walk, not being allowed to visit the dead. No, that year I didn't get to listen to Mamagrande chat with those who came to clean the neighboring tombs, who also were remembering their dead, telling stories of their lives.

⤙ Lucita ⤚

Every year Mamagrande hired a young boy to carry water in a pail to clean the tomb. She also hired one of the sign painters who stood at the entrance soliciting patrons as they came in. Most who came to honor their dead brought fresh flowers, cempoales, chrysanthemums, recedad, jasmines; they also brought wreaths of crepe paper flowers dipped in wax; among the ever-popular roses, the wreaths sometimes sported red hibiscus, yellow and white margaritas, even white calla lilies, and various shades of green-leafed bouquets arranged around a wire frame wrapped in green crepe paper. Many brought the tools they would need to clean the tomb and pull out weeds—a broom, a hoe, of course, a pail for water. But many like Mamagrande preferred to hire someone there to do the job. Then she'd visit with the others, telling stories. One story she always told was of how her youngest daughter María de la Luz was named after her dead Lucita who had been truly beautiful, who would sing like a bird, and who had been killed by a stray bullet. A gypsy had foretold young

72

Lucita's destiny. Mamagrande sitting in the plaza in Laredo, México, after going to Mass at Santo Niño de Atocha church one Sunday, holds Lucita on her lap. When a gitana approaches her and putting her hand on Lucita's head, proclaims "This child shall die young and in tragedy, she'll never know sorrow or pain." Mamagrande tries to plead with the gitana not to place such a curse on the child, but the gitana insists it is not a curse, but the child's destiny, and nothing can be done about it. Mamagrande then lived with such worry that she became overprotective of the child. But with time, she became careless, and that day, like any other, Lucita goes to the corner store with a neighbor girl on an errand. As they pass a neighbor's house the neighbor's son is cleaning his pistol, accidentally fires one shot, the shot meant for her Lucita. It hit her en la cien, killing her instantly. She was twelve years old. Mamagrande never tires of telling the story, crossing herself as she repeats the last words, "y murió al instante."

⌁ Treeky-Treat ⌁

Thirty years later I returned with Tía Nicha on Day of the Dead to clean Buelito's tomb; we visited with her Comadre Adela whose parents were also now buried in the cemetery across the street. As soon as we arrived she sent a grandchild to buy some soft drinks from a house a few doors down, and we drank them readily, thirsty in the November morning heat. The living room, even smaller than I remembered, was packed with flower arrangements at various stages of completion. Yes, she was still making the wreaths, but only on special orders did she still create her most artistic arrangements with the crepe paper flowers dipped in wax (most of her customers preferred plastic—they last longer—and her daughters who were now helping in the business had persuaded her to accommodate her customers). After the visit, Tía Nicha and I made our way to the cemetery, leaving the car there and promising to return for dinner. As in the old days, stands lined the street outside the cemetery; some sold taquitos, enchiladas, corn on the cob, fruit—slices of jícama, pineapple, watermelon kept in a glass case with a block of ice—even the tall sugarcane stalks the color of plums not quite ripe leaned here and there against the wall of the cemetery; some sold flower arrangements, only a few boys were ready and willing to carry water and clean the tombs, and we had to search for almost an hour before we found someone who could repaint the cross and crudely paint the words and dates. Everywhere I turned I saw changes, but the most dramatic change was a very tall Frankenstein figure in full costume, makeup and all, who stood at the gate and handed out flyers announcing a Halloween sale at La Argentina, a nearby store. Street children wore masks, painted faces, ragged clothes over their usual rags, and otherwise disguised themselves, and with outstretched hands asked us for "treekytreet." Día de los muertos had taken on a new meaning.

∿ *Elisa* ∿

In one photo Cousin Elisa sits, or rather poses, sprawled on the sofa. She must be in her twenties—maybe thirties—made up and coiffed just so. In another photo taken sometime before or after, she, Papi, and I stand outside of her sister Chela's Matamoros home. She's holding a nephew in her arms, her hair under a nylon scarf all up on big pink rollers to fight the frizzies. The gulf wind lifts a corner of my shirt. I'm wearing the blue pedal pushers I made and the sleeveless turquoise cotton blouse Mami made for me for the school photo that year. We've come to visit Elisa's sisters Chela and Linda, my two cousins who stayed in Matamoros when the family moved to Saltillo. Elisa's visiting us from L.A. with her brother Wicho who's just married the daughter of a restaurant owner in L.A. He's brought her to meet the family. But that marriage won't last and he'll be back to Monterrey to marry the woman ten years his elder who is related somehow. So we have pictures of Wicho's two weddings. In Matamoros visiting her sister Chela, Elisa's happy, joking and playing with us. Armando, Chela's husband is our host and takes us to the beach, and to a restaurant to eat seafood, big fat shrimp the shrimpers have just caught. And we fall asleep on the floor on colchas listening to the adults talking, soft murmurs, whisperings in the kitchen around the table, drinking coffee. Laughter, loud carcajadas erupt now and then.

Elisa in her daring two-piece black bathing suit plays with us in the sand. She's generous as ever, her voice caresses with soft purrs. I yearn to hear stories of L.A., of her life as a single woman, but we're never alone so I can ask her things. Ten years later, that summer after Tino's killed in 'Nam, I take a vacation from the office job to visit her in L.A. Rosalinda, Elisa's daughter, and Tía Luz and I fly in from San Antonio. The next day I unexpectedly burst into tears as we eat fried chicken. I have no explanation and lie—"It's because I was thinking of so many who don't have any food." But, what makes me cry is Elisa's life, her reality, and Tino's absence; I'm homesick, I miss Laredo, I'm in mourning. We go to Disneyland, visit relatives in Tijuana, traipse through Forest Lawn, take the bus to Santa Mónica Beach where we have what the sign says are Coney Island hot dogs. But through it all, I feel hollow, sad. Rosalinda lives with Tía Tere and Tío Luis in Monterrey; Elisa sends her hard-earned money to pay for private school, for clothes, even for a house they build out in the country near Tía Luz's chicken farm. They set up a small grocery store and a weekend restaurant where they sell beer, barbacoa, and whatever else Tía Tere cooks. Elisa's brothers help, but not much. Wicho, involved with his life; Nando, the intellectual, marries right after graduation, begins teaching at the technológico; her sisters married and living in Matamoros where they all lived for a while; Mundo the youngest off in Mexico City playing at being a Marxist. Elisa, the black sheep, the one Papagrande never forgave, the oldest of the grandchildren, she is my favorite cousin. She who at sixteen was seduced, "salio con su domingo siete" and was ousted by Papagrande from the family. Tío Luis not standing up for his daughter and Tía Tere, rosary in hand, praying night and day, moved the family to Saltillo. Elisa left to L.A. as soon as the child was born. She found family, Andrea, Mamagrande's cousin, and Javier took her in. They had left three older children and come to California seeking help for Samuel their youngest. They'd stayed in L.A. when Samuel finally succumbed to leukemia, not even the latest medical advances in California could help. Why go back? Everything they had, they'd sold to move to California, to give Sammy the very best care. But at age seven he was gone. By then their other children, the oldest ones, had made a way for themselves staying with their aunts and uncles, grandparents, studying. Their daughter married an Iranian and moved to that desert country and only wrote once or twice a year. She visited with the children one time—they couldn't recognize the free-spirited teenager in the solemn, quiet woman whose eyes shone with love for her kids and had spent all her passions on them. Even her name had changed, unrecognizable. Another son, Lalo, became a revolutionary—even went to Cuba— and during the sixties' political upheaval survived Tlatelolco, but he was in such great danger they had brought him to California against his wishes. I met him then in '68 when we both believed fervently that the revolution was imminent: Marxism was the answer, capitalism would soon be a footnote in history books. We read Neruda and exchanged long passionate political letters. Eventually he returned to Mexico and settled in the south where the struggle never died out as it seemed to have in the north. Family. Elisa found family a great help, but a hindrance as well; soon she began working, moved out, got her papers in order. She worked and worked and worked to raise her daughter from afar: not to see her child grow, not to be there for her first step, or her first day at school, or to dry her tears when she fell, or to enjoy her laughter, a far greater punishment as far as she was concerned than being banished from Papagrande's house. Not to be a mother. Elisa didn't marry until her daughter married. And then it was to a Chicano, a widower whose wife had died of cancer, whose children were all grown and gone, who claimed to love her. Yet he never ate restaurant food but waited every evening till she got home from work and cooked and served him his favorite meals. She washed, ironed, and daily laid out his clothes, down to the very handkerchief he would carry that day. She's never stopped working, although she has risen above the minimum wage pay she earned for over twenty years. In the photos of that trip to Matamoros, she's carefree and happy, laughing her movie star laughter, a smile that would burst into howls that brought tears to her eyes. Laughing at my sister Dahlia's accident—the lamp falling on her head gave her a chichón. Laughing at Papi's jokes. Laughing at frizzy hair. At least then, in the sexy photo, she was happy in spite of the sadness.

⤝ Tina One ⤞

It's Tina's quinceañera and we've come from Laredo to Anáhuac to celebrate, and for Mami and Papi to baptize the baby Josefina. In the photo, Pana, Tina's sister, stands in the foreground; Tina's friends and cousins sit and stand around her. A calendar on the wall, the curtains knotted up to let the breeze in. It was Papagrande and Mamagrande's house before they left the parcela to Tío Luis and Tío Polo to run. Left the house in town to Tío Polo, too. For today at least Tío Polo seems to be in a good mood, jovial and laughing, telling jokes and never once embarrassing Tía Cande with his snarls and put-downs that make Mami furious. Tía Cande prepares the fritada from the kid goats Tío Polo slaughtered early that morning, and all the women labor in the kitchen, making tortillas, sopa de arroz, and all the trimmings for the birthday meal. There won't be a dance; Papagrande deems it's too soon after Granduncle Francisco's death in Corpus Christi. Tina's disappointed, but she won't allow it to spoil her day. Mami has combed Tina's hair: slicked back into a tight braid thick as my skinny nine-year-old arm, tied with a pink shiny ribbon to match her dress. The others, cousins, friends, wear permed hair, short bobs with bangs. I too wear bangs, with a frizzy top that Mami permed with the leftover solution from her home Toni. Oblivious to how I look, I feel grown up in my pony tail, and I wear bobby socks and the blue checked skirt with the three rows of black rickrack across the hem. Tina's hard road is still ahead, for only a year later, Tía Cande will die in childbirth on the way to Nuevo Laredo and too late medical attention that could've saved her life. Tina, at sixteen, becomes mother to five, including Mami's ahijada, the baby Josefina whom everyone calls "Pita," and who almost became our little sister. But Tío Polo decides to move to Monterrey, move in with his parents, he and his six—Tina, Chalo, Pana, Chente, Lily, and Pita. And it's a battle that's just begun, for abdicating all responsibility, he'll let Papagrande raise his children. Tío Polo will soon return to Anáhuac and to the parcela where twenty years later his oldest son, Chalo, will die, alone.

⤳ Chalo ⤶

Chalo. Home after living in Dallas, Houston, L.A., and finally Chicago where he'll marry and father three children; he'll come home to live off the land, fleeing someone or something. Searching for something, he'll drink himself to sleep under the stars. "El Diablo," his nickname in Chicago, dead at thirty-four in the back room of the one cantina in Villa Aldama, near Anáhuac. And the day he dies, I think I see him in Laredo crossing Matamoros Street at the corner with San Bernardo. "Look at that guy, there with the beard, he looks just like my cousin Chalo," I tell my friend Emma whose car is in the shop and has asked for a ride. When I get home, I expect Mami to say "Chalo came to visit." Instead she says,

"Your Aunt Luz called from Monterrey; Chalo is dead; tomorrow they'll bring him to Nuevo Laredo for the funeral." And at four o'clock the next day, I arrive to hugs and greetings from cousins I haven't seen in years. Walking in to the Funeraria Sánchez Chapel, I see Tina and the others up front. To the right of the small altar formed by the casket, framed by a few wreaths and flowers, a young priest talks about Chalo's short but exemplary life; obviously no one had told him of Chalo's nickname. There are few tears. I choose not to go up to the front, I don't want to see Chalo's lifeless face. Later I join my parents in the procession as we walk the short distance to the cemetery, I remember Tía Cande's burial. How her mother and her sisters cried and cried. I, too young to understand much, didn't cry, held Mami's hand, and wouldn't stay with the other children, walked between my parents as I do now.

When we arrive at the site, I notice a dusty clear plastic bag, a bundle, nearby. And just when we are handed the red carnation we are to drop into the coffin before it is finally closed, the funeral director notices that the coffin is too big for the space that has been dug. He apologizes for the inconvenience sends a young helper for a pick-axe. When it arrives, he sheds his coat and tie and begins to dig, as sweat forms strangely shaped dark stains on his white shirt. The monuments, low lápidas, cast shadows in the five o'clock sun. In groups, we wait, sitting or standing around. I ask Mami what's in the plastic bundle. "Es tu Tía Cande," she says offhandedly. Pita who is weeping into a piece of kleenex, explains how "los restos" were exhumed earlier that day and how only Tina and Pana were present. I notice a skull and a long bone, perhaps a leg or an arm, and shudder, say a prayer. Chalo is to be buried with his mother. And he is, when the funeral director turned-grave-digger gives the signal, we resume the services, and the priest one last time blesses the body. The plastic bundle is placed at Chalo's feet. I am forced to see the bearded handsome face, notice the hands folded over a rosary as I too drop my red carnation; in my myopia the carnations are bright red tears of blood covering the body. Finally, the funeral director shuts the lid, lowers the casket, signals that we are to walk single-file and take a handful of the dark, newly dug dirt. The sound of dirt hitting the casket does it for me. I wipe teary eyes and dust-blackened hands on a handkerchief Mami hands me.

As we walk back to the car, I suggest we go eat something. Mami agrees, Papi falters, then agrees but only if we go on the other side. Or do they want to go to Tía Cande's family house, talk to people some more. No, we've already said good-bye. No, most of the relatives are going right back to Monterrey, Dallas, San Antonio, to their homes. "It's better this way," Papi says, "Short and swift." And I know they're thinking of Tino's funeral, the waiting, the extended mourning from the day the army sergeant drove up in the army-green Volkswagen, came to our door at 6:00 A.M. on a Monday morning, spewing words they couldn't understand and I didn't want to understand. The waiting. Almost fifteen days later when the sealed coffin arrived at the airbase escorted by Papi's cousin Ricardo, whose swollen face and red eyes from lack of sleep matched Papi's grief. We talk about Chalo over tacos and orange sodas at El Taquito Millonario. As his padrino, Papi had always felt obliged to help him. We had housed him many times as he came and went from Monterrey or Saltillo to Chicago or Dallas.

"Chalo's finally at rest, in peace," Mami says, "My Comadre Cande was spared all the pain." I wonder if it's her pain, her loss, the loss of a child, or the pain of seeing a child travel the wrong path, end up in apparent nothingness, that she's referring to.

"What will happen to his children in Chicago?" Papi wonders. And I know he's aching for the children my brother didn't have, the ones who'd carry his name.

~ Tina Two ~

At Tina's quinceañera, the brothers aren't in the photo, it's only the girl cousins and her friends; they were probably outside with the men. Tina's life takes twists and turns. She ends up in an exclusive suburb of Dallas married to her Monterrey boyfriend, the son of the Protestant minister whose church is two doors down from Mamagrande's Monterrey house on Washington Street, across the Alameda. Her children grown and gone; her sons and daughters almost forgetting their Mexican heritage, but her youngest at the University of Texas discovering her Mexicanidad in Latin American Studies and Chicano activities. Each of Tío Polo's six now has children, and those are marrying and having children; Tía Cande must have her hands full if she's still guarding her family, the way Mami believes, from over there, the place of light that Mami describes when she talks of dying. The place she went to when Rolando, her youngest was born and she died for a few minutes. The place of peace and joy that she left reluctantly because she didn't want her children to be orphans, didn't want me to be burdened with all those children. And she left that place of light and peace to come back and be our mother. It's a sacrifice, each day a gift from God.

~ Bodas de Oro ~

In the family picture for Mamagrande's fiftieth wedding anniversary, Tati and I are the babies on Mamagrande and Papagrande's lap. Mamagrande wears a diadem of seven gold leafs—the number of children still alive—framing her snow-white hair above aquamarine blue eyes. Papagrande looks like Papi looks now, forty-five years later. Several have gone on, Chalo, Tía Lydia, Tío Chuy, Tía Cande, Tío Polo, and many, many more have come to these my relatives of the blue blood, as Mamagrande liked to brag. And those of us who survive lie scattered across the seven seas—

not just all over the United States and Mexico, but even in Europe and Latin America and far-off islands no one remembers the names of. But most have never strayed farther than San Antonio or Monterrey, stayed by the frontera where grandaunts, granduncles, grandparents, great-grandparents, great-great-grandparents have lived and died. There must've been relatives come to celebrate with Mamagrande and Papagrande. Tía Chita and Tía Toña, Mamagrande's maiden sisters; Tía Piedad and Tío Francisco, Papagrande's sister from Mexico City and brother from Corpus Christi. The family. Extending sideways uncles, aunts, cousins; and back into the past parents, grandparents, great-grandparents; and forward children, grandchildren, to today. The Bodas de Oro—golden anniversary celebrating survival, celebrating endurance, celebrating family.

⤙ Tía Chita ⤚

When I see old movies I recall Tía Chita's dictum—"Batallarón, batallarón, pero se casarón," she'd sum up the plots, "They struggled and struggled, but ended up married." Jesusa Vargas, Tía Chita, Mamagrande's older sister. She and Tía Toña were left to dress saints as the saying goes, but they didn't really—I don't recall either one of them being churchgoers. Papagrande may have blasted his cuñadas in other ways, but he could never claim that they ate saints and shit devils as he was wont to say of Epifania their neighbor who not only attended daily mass in the morning and daily rosary in the evening but also helped with two masses on Sunday and yet was known as the biggest gossip in the neighborhood. No, Tía Toña and Tía Chita didn't go to church much. But Tía Chita did wear an escapulario of the Holy Trinity and an eighteen-carat gold medal of the Virgen del Carmen the size of a fifty-cent piece. Never married, solteronas. They lived in the family home in Monterrey. Tía Chita read newspapers religiously, could argue politics with the best of them. She had a mean sweet tooth—loved lemon drops and chocolates as much as viznaga and sugared pumpkin we bought from the dulceros, the Rendóns who made the best leche quemada in all of Monterrey. Tía Chita. The smell of baby powder and gardenias followed and preceded her. She'd put her false teeth on to eat, otherwise she carried her placas in her pocket; the same pocket where she carried two handkerchiefs, one to be used as such and another knotted around bills and coins.

It was in the late sixties, when I got to see her on one of my short weekend trips to Monterrey. She sensed something, for when I left Mamagrande's house that Sunday to take the bus back to Laredo, amidst other good-bye talk, giving me her bendición, she said, "Cuídate, y que dios te bendiga. A lo mejor ya no te vuelvo a ver."

"Ay, Tía no diga esas cosas," I protested.

But she answered, "Ay, hija, a mis años sólo Dios sabe."

She was right. Her sister Tía Toña had passed on. She waited her turn, patiently living with her three cats, innumerable plants, and her memories of a carefree and oppressive youth, in the house on Félix U. Gómez at the corner that now houses a Bancomer.

Tía Piedad

Tía Piedad, Papagrande's sister, lived in Mexico City and because I lived in the United States I was spared the fate of my other older cousins—Tina, Elisa, Lola, and even her youngest niece Luz—who each were recruited to spend time with her and learn to be proper señoritas. She had married twice and was in her own way a scandal, but because of her wealth and her beauty she remained highly regarded, although Papagrande never mentioned her by name but called her "my sister, the crazy one." None of the cousins who went to Mexico City to live with her and to be trained in proper etiquette remained there long, for the regimen was so strict none of them could survive it. First there were lessons on everything from posture and yoga to nutrition and etiquette, and even French. Tía Piedad's book on posture and beauty, published with the help of her French husband, reputedly a very rich descendent of a family of the nobility who had stayed in Mexico after the political debacle of his countrymen, gave the basics, but there was more, much more. The punishments for not sitting properly or for talking out of turn at the table were double the number of posture exercises and a one day fast, respectively. She was living testimony to her strong commitment to beauty and health, and cousins told of her smooth porcelain skin, her shiny dark chestnut hair, her long elegantly gloved pianist hands, her armoires full of clothes for all occasions—evening gowns glittery and billowy as those in the movies, and tailored day suits to be worn with soft-as-baby-skin silk blouses—all "confectioned" by her personal courtier, and her shelf-lined wall that housed her hundreds of shoes, of all different colors imaginable from all over the world. She always wore "complete attire," which meant everything from hats, earrings, and handkerchiefs to her dresses and shoes was planned and executed to create a total effect. She became a figure of mythic proportions, so when I saw the photograph of her and Luz, captured by a street photographer, walking arm in arm on the street across from the Zócalo, I was surprised that she was no taller than Luz, even in her platform shoes. The cousins still laugh at the tantrums they'd throw and the scenes they put her through so that finally Tía Piedad would give up and send them back to their parents en el norte with her regrets, but so-and-so would never be a lady. And Papagrande would laugh and tease and perhaps teach with a dicho, "el hábito no hace al monje," or "de tal palo tal astilla"—but, as Luz still claims, it wasn't worth so much suffering, so much deprivation just to be "a lady." I'm sure I would've failed as well, long thin hands and all. I have never been able to sit straight and prefer to drape my long thin body over chairs and sofas, sometimes my legs find themselves under me or over an arm of a armchair—no, the posture, definitely not. The etiquette, who knows?

The clothes, well, I do love well-made clothes, good fabrics, clothes that fit well. At one time I suffered from a shoe fetish; I owned more shoes than clothes, amassing red, blue, purple, and even green shoes of all styles: flats, sandals, boots, lace-ups, espadrilles, clogs, sling-backs, heels, pumps; shoes made of plastic, regular as well as suede and patent leathers, canvas cloth, or combinations thereof. I don't remember thinking of Tía Piedad then. Of course, that was during a period when I worked in an office and had to wear certain costumes; I even wore a girdle and hose, yes, before pantyhose—a perfect excuse for owning so many shoes. Later I would only own a pair of huaraches for summer and a pair of hiking boots for winter; of course, a much better choice of footwear for my politics and lifestyle, but that was years later, after my office worker life. It may have been a genetic impulse, so I guess I can forgive my excesses in the footwear department; Tía Piedad would've been proud.

And on my book shelf sits her 1962 *Corrección de Postura*, reminding me that both beauty and health are the result of correct posture and proper breathing.

⤳ Christmas ⤳

Christmases past. Some with and some without photos haunt me every December. The year we must've been doing all right with Papi working construction for Zachry and going out of town on jobs. Under the small tree, I couldn't believe my eyes, the Sears Roebuck doll house just like the one in the catalog, and a doll with shiny blonde hair and rosy cheeks. That year we all got two gifts; the many other years when we were laid-off poor and there were no gifts: the year when we didn't have a tree until the very last day of school I won my classroom's tree; the year we didn't have a tree at all until I went and decorated a mesquite branch. I could see Mami's tears beneath her hopelessness, and the younger kids' skepticism, "That's not a tree," one claimed, "Shhh, it's our kind of tree," another answered. Yet, every year, we had a "nacimiento" laid out on Spanish moss on the TV set, the Baby Jesus no bigger than my little finger. The year Mami made us all our gifts: warm slippers from yarn scraps that Doña Carmen had given her. Most years she filled large brown grocery bags with oranges, limes, grapefruits, and pecans from our trees for our neighbors; sent Tino and me to deliver Christmas gifts to the neighbors: Valdezes and the Treviños whose Dad also was laid off from the smelter and who had it even worse than us because of their sick grandmother and a brand new baby, respectively; and smaller bags to Father Jones at San Luis Rey Church and to Doña Carmen and Don Vicente because they didn't have children.

Some years, we went to Monterrey for Nochebuena, riding the train and eating taquitos Bueli had packed for us, staying until past January 6, for that's when the Reyes Magos came. Mamagrande's nacimiento took up a whole room. Tía Luz would set it up in the living room, the figures—St. Joseph, Mary, the baby, even the shepherds and the hermit and the devils—spread out on the Spanish moss. At midnight gunshots exploded everywhere. At midnight Mass, I nodded, but didn't dare fall asleep. And when we went to Monterrey, Santa Claus wouldn't come at all; it was the three Kings who left candy and gifts in the shoes of good little girls on January 6.

And as I grew older, I wanted to give real gifts, store bought and not handmade, for my parents and Bueli, for my friends at school, for my teacher, so I saved pennies from the milk-money Mami would scrape together by sewing, and I tried really hard not to speak Spanish because then the pennies would disappear into the fines for such transgressions. Tino and I sold our translation services: comic books for a nickel; and sometimes we'd sell the answers to homework problems to the lazy but relatively rich amongst us, those who could afford to buy not just plain milk but chocolate milk, which costs three cents more; they could even buy candies from the "tiendita" during recess. And often bribed friendships. We saved our money and bought gifts. A pair of combs for Bueli, perfume for Mami, tobacco for Papi, a ceramic figurine for Tía Nicha, she loved miniature dogs that resembled the scruffy ones in her yard.

↤ Henrietta ↦

One of these "rich ones" was Henrietta, my fourth-grade best friend—she'd been born up north that was why she wasn't "Enriqueta," or worse, plain "Queta" like my cousin. No, she was "Henrietta" and wore immaculate white socks that were never eaten at the heel by her shiny black, freshly polished shoes, that smelled of the thick black paste her Dad used to polish them every night like he had learned to polish his boots in the Air Force. She wore the most beautiful store-bought dresses, and she even had a tiny black patent leather purse where she carried her milk money and a quarter a day for spending money. She didn't know Spanish—so she never had to pay a fine or write lines as punishment for using it. But although she didn't speak Spanish, she understood everything. This, only I as her best friend knew. That's how she found out one day another secret which she immediately shared with me; this secret, however, ended our friendship. When her mother and father were talking Spanish and thought she didn't understand, they had talked about her real Dad, Enrique, who had stayed in Chicago; so it was clear that her Dad wasn't her real Dad, he was a stepfather. I'd only heard of stepmothers from stories, and from Imelda whose mother had died and who had then had a stepmother come into her life, a stepmother as mean and ugly as the ones in the stories. For some reason, I made up my fourth-grade mind that Henrietta had lied, made it all up, just so we wouldn't feel bad that her father treated her so nice and all. We broke our friendship in a ritual screaming match where we almost came to blows, but my other friends intervened. We agreed to fight after school at the empty lot two blocks away where most school fights settled school feuds. All afternoon I fidgeted and couldn't concentrate on the lessons before me. I considered backing out, just not showing up, but finally I decided I had to show up; after all, even Helen, whom the guys feared and called "toro," had agreed to "hacerme esquina," and help me out if need be; but Henrietta never showed up and the group soon dispersed and went home disappointed. On the way home, Chelo, Helen, and I climbed over a six-foot-high chain link fence to get into the backyard of an abandoned, boarded-up house whose owners had not come back from El Norte that year. We walked home, talking about Henrietta, as we peeled and ate the fruit of our labor: the sun-warmed tangerines exploded into juicy tangy sweetness in our mouths; somehow, perhaps because of their origin, they tasted better than the ones from Papi's grafted trees at home. We parted ways, they went in one direction, I in another. As I walked the last three blocks home alone, I kept pulling my socks up because my shoes kept "eating them up" at the heel. I also thought of the two new sins I had to confess on Saturday to Brother Joseph, who had come to help Father Jones: stealing and fighting. When I got home, tore off shoes and socks, saw the dirty orange-stained heels of my white socks, I thought of how Henrietta's socks would never look like that. I think I loved her.

ᴖ Outings ᴖ

Some Sundays, before we were too many children, Mami and Papi would take us to hear Mass in Nuevo Laredo at Santo Niño de Atocha. After Mass we either went to a restaurant—El Alma Latina or El Cadillac, that is, when there were only two or three of us. As the family grew restaurants became out of the question (we were too rowdy, and it was too expensive to feed so many) but not Sunday outings. Off we'd go to Parque Viveros, where we ate taquitos de carne adobada, made with the fresh tortillas bought from the tortilleras at the Mercado, stacks of tortillas wrapped in white or sometimes just plain brown butcher paper. Papi would buy a kilo of meat from Don Luis, a kind and jovial prankster who'd slice the meat from the roast thin and juicy onto a piece of pink butcher paper and weigh it on a scale everyone joked was "fixed." That and whatever seasonal fruit—mangoes, oranges, bananas, watermelon, even strawberries—was our lunch. We devoured it all. Hungry as pups, after playing on the jungle gym or if it was too crowded just playing a la roña, or a las escondidas, while Mami, Papi and Bueli sat under a shady pecan tree talked and watched us play. Years later, we were too many for even those outings, and we settled for sporadic "picnics" at Easter or on a nice—not too hot—spring Sunday. Picnics at Lake Casa Blanca meant wading barefoot in the shallow edges, being scared of "robachicos" when you went to the bathroom, and playing against each other skipping stones—especially selected flat ones. The photos all reveal hot and sweaty kids too eager to return to interrupted games, nervously posing for Papi or Mami and the Brownie.

Easters were special, with the confetti-filled cascarones that Tía Luz had helped dye and prepare. Eggshells we'd saved for months, and painstakingly decorated were gone in a matter of minutes, shattered over or on someone's unsuspecting head. Of course, we were all expecting it so we ran and chased around, until even the adults joined in the fracas. Picnic food could be anything from bologna sandwiches and Kool-Aid from a thermos to fried chicken and bottles of soft drinks bought across by the case—amber-colored, sweet-tasting cider, sparkly lemon-lime, sugary pineapple, and a tingly orange tasting soft drink, in addition to the usual Coke; saving the bottles so as to get a refund, or so as not to have to pay a deposit on the next case. We didn't always need an excuse for a picnic or at least a drive out to the lake. Some afternoons, Papi would get home from the smelter smelling of metal and sweat, his grey union suit turned black with soot, his black lunch box empty except for the delicious odors of what it had housed earlier. We'd beg for a ride— "un rait, un rait," we'd shout and hold on to his arms, his legs, like lichen. We always seemed to know when to persist, and on those occasions, he'd shower in the makeshift shower stall with the thin black snake of a hose, change into regular clothes, and off we'd go. We'd all pile into the green Ford, later the grey Nash, and much later into a red-and-white, '55 Chevy and off we'd go, fighting for the windows. Sometimes I won, and didn't care if it really was Tino's turn: making faces against the wind, taking big gulps of wind, and feeling the breeze whip my hair against my face. At the lake he'd sit with Mami on the pebbled beach talking while we played, till the sun, a giant orange balloon, disappeared in the west.

Time to go home, do homework, make dinner—perhaps potatoes and eggs, fried beans (we'd had the boiled ones, en bola) for lunch, and of course the flour tortillas Bueli was making. And tea—orange blossom, orange leaf, lemon grass, cinnamon, or yerbabuena—with milk and sugar, if you liked. Papi had been up since five-thirty and attended Mass at six and then gone to work at seven just as we were getting up: "Arriba todo género pichicuate!" he'd call to wake us up, although usually his singing De Colores in full voice and off key when he returned from Mass had probably already done it. By the time he returned from Mass, Mami had fixed his breakfast; his lunchbox on a back burner, waited like a patient pet, black and warm. After Bueli died, whenever Mami had had a baby or was sick, I prepared his lunchbox—packing the leftovers from the previous night's dinner into taquitos—we didn't call them "mariachis" then as they do now in Laredo—fresh flour tortillas stuffed with picadillo, a spicy ground-beef dish, or Mexican sausage with egg, or sometimes, just plain beans; the hot coffee from the pot he'd prepared earlier, filled the silver-colored thermos with the red top that became a cup. On the school bus, I'd still be cleaning dough from under my fingernails, going over homework, or reading—Corin Tellado, Agatha Christie from home, or whatever was the current book on my library project—I intended to read every single book in our meager junior high library; I only got to the M's when the school year ended.

↜ *Summer Reading* ↝

In the summer, we didn't stop reading just because we didn't have access to the school library—there was still the public library downtown, and all the magazines and books "El Viejo," Papi's boss at the smelter, was going to throw away and Papi brought home for us—Reader's Digest Condensed Books, *Life* magazine, and comic books. Because Papi did odd jobs around their house on weekends, carpentry and such, El Viejo gave him things they discarded—furniture, clothes, and books. One year Papi brought an ottoman, a box filled with black clothes, and a year's worth of *Life* magazine. We had a ball. One summer, right before school started, my parents bought the World Book Encyclopedia from a teacher who was going door to door; Tino and I rejoiced, although we knew what sacrifice it was for them—three years of weekly payments. We revered the blue bound volumes. And we begged to get the annual supplement that had more recent material. We knew there was plenty to read and to memorize—like the states and their capitals, both the U.S. and Mexico—even during the summers when schools shut down and the afternoons stretched as long as Saunders, the street that became the highway to Corpus Christi and the beach. We wanted to know it all. One summer Tino and I discovered mysteries and science fiction. But of course there were other things to do; not everything happened in books.

⤙ La Escuelita ⤚

The summer before seventh grade, I opened my own escuelita, charged twenty-five cents per child. Taught five- and six-year-olds and a couple of mature four-year-olds, all about school—in English and Spanish, nursery rhymes, alphabets, numbers, and games, some I'd learned from my cousins in Monterrey others from school—

"Naranja dulce, limón partido, dame un abrazo que yo te pido; María Blanca está encerrada en pilares de oro y plata, romperemos un pilar para ver a María Blanca.

Vamos a ver los quehaceres de la vida.

Here we go round the mulberry bush.

You put your right hand in, you put your right hand out, you do the hokey pokey and you turn yourself around, that's what it's all about," which really didn't make any sense to me or to my young charges who didn't speak or understand a word of English.

I felt grown up and successful for had I not just taught Doña Carmen her citizenship questions? And she had passed, too. I was making money, $2.50 a week, without having to get up at four in the morning to go pick cotton. But my business was short-lived. Because of an accident, I had to close the school and send the children home. We were burning trash in the backyard. It was late evening, the crickets singing, the birds finding their perch for the night, and we had already burned most of the pile— mostly dry leafs and scraps of paper. I stood in the dusky light at the very back of the yard, by the privy, rake in hand contemplating the nap of the smooth, even broomstrokes that looked like velvet after you pass your hand over it, enjoying the fire that noisily crackled as it gobbled up paper and twigs and leaves and made them disappear into blackness. Suddenly I heard a loud pop, like a firecracker. I felt the pain sharp as bright light and saw the blood running down my leg. Bueli, who was watering the fruit trees on the other side, had been hit, too. She cried out, "¡Ave María Purísima!" We never did find out who had broken the rule and tossed a hair spray can into the pile of things to burn. I had to wear a bandage, and I winced when I walked. Mami thought I better close the school, so I did. Because I couldn't handle Bueli's old Singer without pain, I embroidered and crocheted, hemmed and made button holes, helping Mami sew the school clothes for ourselves and for her encargos. I had learned to sew on the machine at age nine, making underwear for the preschoolers Esperanza and Margie. By junior high I was making some of my own clothes as well as helping Mami with her own sewing. Mami never used a pattern, so when in homemaking I had to use one, I was confused. The empire waist on the sapphire blue chintz dress with the side-zipper never did fit as well as if I'd used Mami's method, but I got an "A" on the project.

A few weeks after my accident, Tía Chacha came through on the way to Monterrey from Chicago. I was sent to spend the rest of the summer with Mamagrande in the cool house on Washington Street. I never mentioned the accident; I didn't want sympathy. The scar's hardly visible—a thin line drawn with a chalk or slab of soap on brown skin like the designs Mami and Bueli draw on the cotton sateen for quilting colchas. The scar remains slightly less visible than the heart shaped birthmark on my thin brown calf.

↜ La Cueva ↝

Not all summers were spent sewing, reading, or in Monterrey, though. One summer we spent digging out a cave in an area behind our house, beyond the outdoor privy. "El monte," shaded by huge cedar ash trees and full of mesquite and huisache brush, harbored legions of bugs and larger animals—horned toads, lagartijos, spiders, chicharras, even snakes, so naturally we loved to play in the wilds of el monte. Actually, the pit we called our cave had initially been dug by Tío Simón who swore he had seen a fire the size of a man right on that spot and had begun to dig looking for the treasure he knew was buried there. But he and his family had left for El Norte in April and so we inherited the idea of the treasure and the pit. Tino, our neighbor Eleazar, and I had read enough pirate stories; we knew all about treasures. So we organized ourselves into digging teams—mornings, it was Raúl, Eleazar, and Marcos—their sisters Nana and Rosa were too young and were not admitted, neither were our youngest sisters, Espy and Margie. Pedro, Carmela, and Quico, but not their youngest sister Tina, dug in the afternoons. Tino, Dahlia, and I spent all our time at the pit since it was practically in our backyard. Lalo our cousin had left with Tía Nicha and Tío Güero p'al Norte or he'd have been there too. How surprised he'd be when he got back and saw our treasure! We had grandiose schemes for what we would do when we found the buried riches. We also discussed the digging: what if we found a skeleton, maybe an Indian that had died or been killed? Or what if we found a mastodon or a dinosaur? Or what if we kept on digging and digging until we reached the center of the earth? What would we find? Fire? Water? Or could we keep digging and not know how far we were until we got to the other side of the earth? Would we be in China? Eleazar consulted a map, and informed us it would be Africa, but we didn't all agree and since we didn't have a globe we couldn't be sure. "What if we reached Hell and angered the Devil?" asked Carmela. None

95

of us wanted to deal with that one. But after about a week we tired of digging and digging and not finding anything except hard-packed earth and a few fist-size stones and even an arrowhead now and then. Papi teased that he would hire us out to dig privies. We finally gave up. We abandoned the dig, but not the site; after all we had made a tremendous headway from where it had been when Tío Simón left. It was even bigger, and cooler, than the old rusty green car that had been our favorite hide-away in the nearby dump. It would become our new hideaway, our cueva for secret meetings and for special ceremonies. Which meetings or cere-monies, we never specified. We often scavenged the nearby cascajera for furniture and treasures for our cave. We each had an old tire, also sal-vaged from the dump, which served many purposes: you could roll it around and it was your car, or you could squeeze a younger and willing sibling into it and give her or him a ride. In our cowboys and Indians games, the tires became wagons on a wagon train. When the heat over-came us and we just wanted to sit and loll around like tired cows, we took them to the cave and sat on them talking, making up stories of UFOs and witches who could read your mind. We'd start with silly things and eventually get to serious stuff—the younger kids would leave, probably bored, but Eleazar, Pedro, and I would stay and talk, deep as religion— we pondered Sister Consuelo's choice for us: "if the communists came and asked if you believed in Jesus, what would you do? Now, remember, if you say you believe in Jesus, they'll kill you." Talk serious as death. Where is Martha's Mamagrande? Did she really sing with the angels? When they buried you and the bugs ate your skin and your body, could you feel anything? Talk, rational and questioning as science: why can you see the lightning before you hear it? What makes the sky blue and rain-bows full of colors? Why do rainbows appear on soap bubbles? We pon-dered all these and many more and even tried a number of experiments in our cave: how long would cicadas live without wings? Did salamanders grow their tails back, like fingernails? My own experiment involved coffee grounds. Every morning when I'd wash the coffee pot, I'd collect the grounds in an old can. When I'd saved enough, I'd conduct the experiments—I dyed my doll's blonde hair with the liquid made with distilled syrup from the grounds and the gummy resin from the mesquite tree. Although most of our experiments were pretty safe, there were some that we thought dangerous. One such experiment involved fire. I thought Eleazar and Pedro were playing checkers, but later I found out that they had amassed firecrackers and were making a bomb. The fire got away from them. They barely got out after the explosion, just barely before the fire consumed all our prized possessions: my wooden box with the carved angel on the lid; my button collection; Tino's baseball cards; Eleazar's comic books, his pirate's knife; shoe boxes and hat boxes, boxes large and small—all the boxes we'd amassed and filled—each one of us with treasures great and small. The hungry fire raged tall as a man as it took everything—the old curtains that served as flooring; "coja," the old rocking chair that was missing a leg; and Mami's blue chenille robe with the roses down the front, so worn that the cuffs and the neck ridges had smoothed into soft sheer cotton, and which I had taken to wear when I was alone in the cave, finding comfort in the Mami smell of it. When Tío Simón returned in October wanting to get back to his digging, Papi teased him and told him that, yes, there had been a fire big as man on the very site. "And it took our treasures!" but I didn't dare let on how much it hurt. I laughed with everyone at Tío Simón's boasting that he could see into the future. "¡A qué huercos carajos!" was all he said when he heard the full story of the experiments.

⌁ The Fire ⌁

Of course there were other fires. We were still living on Santa María when the Chavira family lost everything, including the two-month-old baby, to a fire started by a lightning bolt. The flames reached to the sky.

Bueli had covered all the mirrors with white sheets and had unplugged the radio, the iron, the lamps; as soon as she heard thunder, she checked every plug in the house that might draw the deadly bolts from the sky. The Chavira's house. We can hear the fire, we can see the flames, could hear the crying and Locha's screams. Neighbors rush over, try to help. Tino and I remain safe with Bueli while Mami and Papi go see what can be done. I had nightmares, nightmares of fire, and of burning babies. In one, a rag doll—blonde on one side and black on the flipside—became my brother and had caught fire. I woke up screaming, next to Bueli, in her cot. She hushed me. Amid sobbing, I told her what I'd seen. She led me to the crib where my brother laid. "See, he's okay, and here's your doll, it's okay too. You just had a pesadilla." The next day she and Mami agreed I needed to be healed de susto.

⌁ Susto ⌁

Susto. Espanto. It happened. Another time, Mami had mistaken the dark brown bottles of the baby's vitamin drops for Bueli's eyedrops. Bueli cried and screamed in pain; Mami cried and screamed in fright, and I cried and screamed not knowing what was going on. Tía Nicha rushed to get a neighbor to take Bueli to the doctor. All was well, but I stopped eating, was feverish, had yellow nails, and turned pale and sickly. Mami took me to Doctor del Valle in Nuevo Laredo who prescribed a series of shots to be given daily for eight days. I was jaundiced. Had a severe infection. But even after the long bus trips to get the shots and more trips to the doctor's office with the calendar with the print of the Indian woman cradling a sick child, even after all that, I still didn't want to eat and grew thinner. The fevers disappeared but not the bad dreams. There was only one solution: a healing for fright. Bueli asked a neighbor to come and pray over me. The warm smell of pirul engulfed me and I was to reply three times, "ay voy," when Doña Cipriana called to me, "Vente Azucena, no te quedes" after mumbling prayers to herself. I did as I was told and got well.

⁓ *Romana* ⁓

The second fire I witnessed didn't scare me so much. We were already on San Carlos Street when Romana's house, a block away in the backyard of her sister Jovita's more affluent home, burned one night. They'd built the outdoor fire to keep warm too close to the two-room frame house where Doña Lupe and her daughter Romana and her children lived amid piles of clothing and rags. Because they cooked in an outdoor oven and over an open fire, and didn't even have gas or electricity in their tiny house, they always smelled of burned mesquite, their clothes stained with soot. That night we all heard the swooshing sound of the fire and saw how the flames lit up the whole neighborhood; even our yard and the empty one next to us was lit up like day. There were few neighbors to help. It was Friday night, even Papi was gone to the cantina. Jovita's husband Eusebio was gone, too, when it happened so it was mostly women and children crying and trying to put out a fire with one garden hose. By the time the firefighters arrived with the siren wailing like in the movies, the little house had been totally destroyed. Doña Lupe screamed at Romana that it was God's punishment for what she was doing. And the neighbors, embarrassed and not knowing what to say, ambled on home. The next day we went to leave some clothes and dishes Mami had put in boxes and bags for the family. Doña Carmen had asked that we kids take her contributions, too. It was like a procession, all morning people coming to help clean the rubble and to deliver whatever they could spare from their own meager belongings to help Romana and her kids, Pola, Carmela, and Pedro. The family would grow to eight before she got wise and either got on the new-found pill or she stopped seeing Eusebio. Unlike her mother Doña Lupe and her sister Jovita, who attended daily Mass

99

and wore escapularios around their necks and seemed to always have rosaries in their hands, Romana only stepped inside the church when she got her kids baptized. "Doña Lupe herself had her daughters from different men," Panchita confided to Mami during her weekly visit that Monday after the fire, "Maybe it was God's punishment to her that her daughters share a husband."

Mami shooed me away, "This is grownup talk, go clean the beans for tomorrow."

I went into the kitchen and as I poured cupful after cupful of pinto beans on the white laminate table and spread them out with my left hand, picking out pebbles, pieces of dirt, even oddly shaped or odd colored beans with the right, I pondered what I'd just heard. Were these the fires of Hell that Sister Consuelo talked about? Did God always punish with fire? What kind of sins were these I had never heard about? Why would God punish saintly Doña Lupe who knew all the prayers by heart and led the novena rosaries when Martha's Mamagrande died with her holy-sounding voice just like the nuns'? I thought about all this as I cleaned the beans, putting the clean ones in the gallon-sized blackened belly jarro, to be rinsed and cooked. On the radio, Ramoncita Esparza interviewed housewives between commercials: for headache, "mejor, mejora Mejoral," and "remoje, enjuage, y tienda," the jingle for Fab detergent instructed. Mami and Papi baptized Romana's Sylvia only two years after the fire, so I guess the punishment didn't take.

⤳ El Mercado ⤵

"Mercado Maclovio Herrera," I remember reading the huge sign, at age four, when Bueli was teaching me to read using El Diario. When the mercado burned, I took a picture of the charred ruins. One of Mami's stories is of how I got lost in the mercado, and they found me with Ruperto the butcher, sitting up high on his refrigerator, but just below the San Jorge image, waving a red lollipop in my hand like a conductor to "Granada," which blared from the radio. Ruperto, our neighbor, single and very handsome, according to Mami, loved me. He teased Papi calling him "suegro," although I was only two. "He'd wait for me," he joked. Papi didn't like such jokes; maybe he sensed that he'd have eight daughters and be "suegro" over and over and over. Mami tells of how one day she and Ruperto were sitting on the front steps playing with me; Papi was just inside the screen door reading the paper, when Cayetano, the new mail carrier arrived to deliver the mail.

"What a beautiful child, and she looks so much like her father," he said, looking at Ruperto.

Mami tells that she turned all colors and Ruperto laughed, but Papi was not amused. Cayetano, the poor cartero, mortified to discover his mistake, apologized over and over, as Papi emerged from inside the house and took me from Mami's arms.

The mercado. Rangel who always made funny jokes and called us pochas, sold us trinkets when we'd save our pennies or a madrina had been generous. Colorful toy baskets filled with tiny pottery that fit small ones into larger ones; I'd imagine how many it would take and what it would be like to see them go on and on expanding, smaller ones into larger ones, until they all fit in Bueli's cazuela for making fritada, a clay pot big as the washtub with the black bottom from sitting on the fire on wash days; tiny pots for tiny meals we'd feed the chicharras; tiny brooms and mops, to clean matchbook size rooms; sometimes, the baskets also came with a doll family so small, the baby was the size of an ant. You couldn't really see through the red or green or blue cellophane anchored with a rubber band to keep prying little fingers out until you got home. Rangel also sold rolling pins and molcajetes along with the toys—valeros, lotería games, tops, pirinolas, masks that made you look just like El Santo or the other wrestlers on TV, and genuine leather whips like the real vaqueros used, like Zorro's.

Rangel's brother, whom we also called Rangel, owned the store on Santa María Street, the store with the popsicle orange walls, so that motorists could see it a mile away, he said. And they did. We did.

Three bells ring when I open the screen door with the aluminum sign I can't read: "Rainbo Bread." I hand Rangel the coins wet with sweat from holding them tight in my three-year-old fist; I repeat Mami or Bueli's "encargo"—sal, harina, manteca, cebolla, huevos, or even pan dulce for the merienda—more than three items and I'd forget, start crying.

↶ *First School* ↷

Santa María had been the main highway north to San Antonio until the developers arranged for San Bernardo to become the motel strip during the fifties. But that would come later, when we lived there, and I was sent to Rangel's to fetch whatever Mami urgently needed. Santa María served as a highway, and cars raced north to San Antonio, south to the bridge and to Mexico. Across Santa María was an elementary school I dreamed of attending: Santa María Elementary. But I wasn't old enough, so I had to cross an empty field where the elementary kids played during recess to Sra. Piña's escuelita. Going to Rangel's wasn't so scary, after all I didn't have to cross Santa María, but going to school meant crossing both the street highway and an empty block. Bueli would watch—I could see her waving far, far away, as I turned to wave before going in to Sra. Piña's house. And at noon she'd be there waiting for me again. We'd repeat our ritual in the afternoon, and when I'd come in around three she'd serve me galletas morenas or marías bought at Rangel's. Or maybe animal crackers or marranitos, my favorite pan dulce, the ginger flavor making my mouth tingle, with milk or chocomilk. I'd sit at my child-size table and chair and tell of all I'd learned: numbers, letters, shapes, poems, new words for things—all in Spanish. Some afternoons we had sugar tortillas, tortillas de azúcar, for our merienda. Even now Mami will sometimes surprise us with a batch of tortillas de azúcar, crispier and as tasty as any pan dulce, that melt in your mouth and leave a cinnamony aftertaste.

∽ Santa María ∾

On quiet evenings, Santa María, the highway to San Antonio, was our entertainment as we sat listening to the radio and watching cars go by. One Saturday afternoon Papi is showing off his new apple-green Ford to Compadre Daniel, Tino's padrino. The two families, Comadre Mary, and Compadre Daniel, their kids Danny and Memo; Mami, Papi, my brother, and I, get in the car. Papi drives back and forth on Santa María. All huddled, feeling the thrill of speeding in the car. A siren scares us. Papi stops and yes, the police officer asks for his license. But Papi sweet-talks him into letting him go with a warning—"Andamos estrenando carro, so we were testing it," he says.

"Bueno, if you say you're estrenando and you're only testing it, but be sure not to drive that fast, okay?"

We're only two blocks from the house. In silence Papi drives on the side street and parks the car. Later they're all laughing at how we were testing the car. For many years later when Mami wants to make him slow down on the road she'll remind him that he isn't estrenando anymore.

That was the same green Ford Mami was driving when she accidentally backed out without shutting the passenger door. Papi was screaming. His anger turned the veins along the neck so big and purple I thought they would explode right out of his skin. And from that day on Mami said she wouldn't drive and he would have to take her everywhere. And he has for these forty-odd years, driven her everywhere from long trips to visit family in Monterrey and to the beach in Corpus to short everyday kind of trips—trips to the mall or the grocery store and to her "distracción," bingo games. First at San Luis Rey Church where Papi as a member of the Holy Name Society gets to call out the numbers loud

103

and clear, while we play a la roña and fall asleep on the folding chairs, underneath light bulbs strung along thin wires lighting the outdoor games. Now to Border Bingo, the commercial hall, where hundreds from both Laredos play, sitting solemnly side by side at tables set row upon row. Before the games begin or between games while the ushers verify the winning card, Mami jokes and chats with her comrades; Mine confides her son is getting divorced; Susana's daughter just found out she's got cancer; Tina's son-in-law was caught with drugs; Concha comes by to say hello, catch up on things; players all around eat frito pies, bemoan their bad luck, and rearrange good luck charms—ivory, jade, bone, wooden elephants of all sizes but always with their trunks up, Buddhas in all sizes, "fixed" garlic cloves tied with red ribbons, images of St. Anthony, or personal favorites such as Santa Teresita or San Martin de Porres, or good luck rosemary and lavender herbal oils sprinkled on themselves and the cards. Amulets—some wrapped in soft red felt, others just stashed away in plastic baggies—put away in pockets, purses, or tote bags until the next time. And Papi waits for the Bingo Monster to spew out the patrons like used fodder every night at ten, and drives her home.

↝ Dahlia Two ↜

In the picture Tía Nicha walks down the front steps of the house on San Carlos Street, and Dahlia stands by the round table that holds her chocolate birthday cake, three candles lit. The wind blows Dahlia's yellow organdy dress, and her short, straight hair frames her round face, big brown eyes, a smile wide as her face; and Tía Nicha's gasp, an inspiration of air, but fast, a sucking "eeeh" and "¡Qué bárbara, ¿Porqué no me dijeron?!" I stand next to Mami when she takes the picture, feel the sun hot on my back, like putting on a cotton slip still warm from Bueli's iron on a cool morning. Tía Nicha who feared having TB, who married Tío Güero in Laredo when she still had a novio, Cayetano, the mail carrier in Nuevo Laredo. She sews, puts up a permanent garage sale, selling dis-

105

cards from all her nieces. Her son drinking himself to a future like his Dad's. Tío who wooed her away from a serious man, a formal man. Tío, who's never sober, yet's never been arrested for DWI; the police know him, bring him home, and the next day his son or a neighbor will take him to retrieve the car. Tío and she newly married when I was born. He went to get the doctor from the billiards table that cold January morning; the doctor wouldn't come because he was winning. Tía Nicha stayed with Mami, Bueli worried. Papi betting that I was a boy, would've paid eighty pesos more if I'd been born a boy. The doctor lost; Papi says, I saved eighty pesos, would've won either way.

Dahlia se carcajea, loud gulps of laughter—it's her birthday picture. Is she laughing at Tía? At me? At Life?

～ *The Wedding* ～

In their wedding pictures Mami looks serious, Papi joyous; they've been married but a few hours. They come to the photo studio straight from Padre Lozano's words pronouncing them "marido y mujer."

He: Jorge Negrete looks—black wavy hair slicked back, trimmed moustache, hazel grey eyes. Wondering what life holds for him; he'd waited till he was twenty-nine to be sure he'd found the right woman to be the mother of his children; that's what worries him, his mother's disapproval and yet he's so sure; and his father's obstinate request; and what about her mother, whom he likes and respects, Doña Celia, where will she go?

She: movie-star beautiful, María Félix eyes, wondering what will happen to her mother, and how he's ten years older and wondering if this is the right thing, knowing it is, but doubting nonetheless; worries about his family's objections and his father's unreasonable insistence that they live at the parcela for a year.

The wedding's gone as planned; her trousseau from Hachar's, the fancy department store in Laredo, exactly what she had wanted, even the florist had come through with her request for calla lilies for her bouquet. All the padrinos arrived on time; the music's professional, the Ave María in church, the dance tunes at the dance. It's the wedding they've dreamed and planned, but still nagging doubts, fears—monsters that plague them even as they settle for the night in the glow of early dawn, la noche de bodas. Azhares, orange blossoms milky white, hold the Spanish lace mantilla on her head. The matching lace bodice, the fifty tiny satin-covered buttons down the back and seven more on each sleeve down to the wrist. November. Not a good month for a wedding. Could rain and ruin everything. Could turn cold. But it doesn't. Stars shine in the clear, crisp night, and it's a good wedding, a good marriage.

◡ Tía Nicha ◠

Seventy years ago, the five-year-old child poses in a canoe at the lake in the park in San Antonio, an oar in her tiny hands. The park photographer with his box up on a tripod set it up just so. On her head, a red bow as big as her father's hand; she looks comfortable in her traje marinero, with the white sailor collar edged with red and blue piping. The water placid as a bed freshly made, the sound of the birds flying overhead, distract her; "No, turn over here, mira, mira." She turns to see a mother duck and her ducklings waddling by where her father stands. The ducks go into the water, swimming effortlessly. "Mira, mira," he calls to her; she looks at him, she hears a click as a light flashes. "¡Ya!" her father says and pulls the canoe in by a rope. He takes her in his arms and they walk away, her mother limping from the recent injury to her hip, her baby sister in a stroller. Tía Nicha remembers as she holds onto the photo and cries.

Why do you cry, Tía?

Because we were so happy.

"Were you?"

"We were. I'm not sure if Mamá was, Father was seeing another woman. No one was supposed to know, but the neighbors came with their gossip and Mamá was heartbroken. The neighbors swore the other woman had put a curse on Mamá, had given her the injury that came from nowhere, the injury that made her limp like an old woman. It was brujerias shrinking her leg, drying up the muscles. In her shortened skirts it was even more visible, so she returned to her old-fashioned skirts long and heavy. She gave away some new fashionable dresses and skirts Papá had had made for her, gave them away to her friend the black woman who lived across the street. She would sit out on the porch rocking the baby to sleep, waiting for Papá, smoking cigarettes, one after the other. I would fall asleep . . ."

"Bueli smoked?"

"Yes, maybe that's why she got the cancer."

"And you had black neighbors in San Antonio?"

"Yes, and Chinese, too; we all lived together, those who worked for the railroad, in the same barrio. Like family. If one was in trouble the others helped out. If Mamá needed an onion when she was cooking she'd send me next door or across the street to borrow one. You can't see it but, I have a doll in the boat with me.

"A doll?"

"Yes, Papá had given us each a doll—your mother and me. They were beautiful handmade cloth dolls with embroidered red lips and blue eyes under black lashes. Later Mamá took them, hid them from us, probably threw them away, or gave them to someone."

"Why?"

"No sé, probably because she thought they were part of the sorcery. As a child, she lived next door to a bruja in Monterrey, you remember the story—how one day when her grandmother who raised her was sleeping her siesta, Mamá couldn't sleep, and instead went outside to play. While playing with her dolls in the zaguán, she heard noises in the yard next door; she peeked through a crack in the wall and saw the bruja, Doña Remedios, I believe she was, burying some beautiful dolls. You have to remember that Mamá was a lonely little girl; she didn't have anyone to play with, and the viejita, her grandmother, was pretty old, so she entertained herself as best as she could. Well, as soon as the bruja had gone back inside, Mamá climbed the wall, dug up the dolls, and brought them to her yard to play. When her grandmother woke up and went to see what the child was doing, she found her in the yard under the willow tree, serving tea to an array of strange homemade dolls with straight pins stuck all over their bodies. She knew immediately what had happened and instructed the child to go back and put the dolls where she had found them or something terrible would happen. Mamá did as she was instructed and never forgot the lesson, for as punishment, the grandmother took all her good dolls too and didn't let her play with dolls for a long, long time.

The tears have stopped for the little girl in the canoe, happy to be so cherished, so protected.

I pick up another photo—Buelito as a young man his right foot on one end of the running board of the Ford and a teddy bear on the other end.

"How Papá loved his car!" Tía exclaims. "He was so proud of his truck, too. I think that's what hurt him most when we left San Antonio; he sold the green car and bought a black pickup truck so we could bring all our furniture, everything back to Mexico. I don't think he minded losing everything as much as he minded losing the truck." And I sense she's near tears again.

110

"Tía, no llore."

"It's the memories; when you're old, you'll cry too, like me, remembering. Or maybe you won't, with your so many trips, you'll have some beautiful remembrances. But, you can see I cry even for the beautiful memories."

Tía Nicha puts the photo back in the shoe box with the other photos and greeting cards—Christmas, friendship post cards, birthday wishes, Mother's Day, birth announcements, a stork holding a bundle announcing the birth of babies to her nieces, nephews. She holds and reads the messages, fingers lovingly invitations to weddings; graduations, yellowed white and formal; esquelas announcing the passing of a friend, a relative—from the time when they were sent black-edged white envelopes send shivers down my back. Her sighs retumban in my heart as I walk down the periwinkle-lined path to my car, her six dogs at my heels, and at my arms, and legs—licking, smelling, sniffling, whining for attention. My mother's sister holds her memories to her chest, sighs, cries, and chuckles as I wave and say, "Ya no llore."

"You'll see, ya verás, when you are old and cry, ya verás, there's solace in tears."

111

⤝ Kites ⤞

Kites. Huilas or Papalotes. Competitions to see which fly the highest and the longest; we always win, Tino and I. For our huilas and papalotes fly higher, caressing the sky way past when the others come crashing down—we could send up to ten letters on one string, they were so high—the longest tails made from scraps from Mami's sewing. We collect branches and cut limbs off the mesquite in the backyard. Then Papi lets us use his knife that folds into the black wood handle. "Mucho cuidado," he cautions. We carefully trim the chosen branches to the desired length and carve a tiny notch at each end where the string fits snugly. We gather newspapers, cut the outline about an inch bigger than the frame. Preparing the frame is only half the job; cutting the paper just so and making sure the string fits, taut as a lampshade, glued on just so, not too much paste and not too much fold on the paper. In the kitchen with Mami or Bueli's help, we cook the flour-based engrudo, over low heat to get the desired consistency, thick as oatmeal atole but smooth as cream-of-wheat; the same paste that Comadre Adela and her daughters use when making crepe paper flowers, the same glue Don Cipriano, the piña-tamaker, uses even now. Each one makes her or his own kite, first choosing: the six-sided huila or the four-sided papalote. The older, more experienced ones choose to make huilas, the younger choose papalotes; older ones helping younger kids, except the ones who cry like Margie who wouldn't let anyone touch her work—theirs won't fly, too heavy with paste or the paper and string not taut. We set our creations out to dry overnight. The next day the huilas and papalotes take flight just like their names indicate. After attaching the tail made from the scraps of the cotton flour sacks Mami would use to make the little ones underwear or summer frocks, we tie one end of the string, wound into a skein the size of a small loaf of bread. Ready. With the wind's collaboration, away from the cubreviento, the tall cedar ash tree in the backyard, and away from

112

the power lines that could really mess up a masterpiece, our kites take flight, like so many birds let loose from their cages. The adults come out to see the kites; sometimes they too write letters on pieces of theme paper. What to write? Prayers to God, to the angels. Papi sends Mami letters. The scraps of paper get smaller and smaller as they rise along the string curving in the wind up, up, up toward the kite barely visible with the long tail swerving, keeping it afloat. Whitish newsprint kites against a blue sky, disappear, are gone in the photo. But I know they're there, flying high above the world. We're in the field by the railroad tracks that run by the dump, my skirt blowing in the wind, Leo and Papi are out there with us; must've been ten kites flying that day. But I remember only mine, and the wind and my kite pulling, pulling at me so I think I'm going to be picked up and sent up like a letter to God. And Mami taking the picture, the wind blowing her hair everywhere.

～ Matachines ～

We walk three blocks to Mother Cabrini Church along with neighbors and compadres. We arrive just as the mayordomo is beating the drum. Pom, pom. Pom, pom. Solemnly calling the dancers who are trickling into the area. The music begins: accordion, violin, and the incessant drumming: tan, tan tatan; tan, tan tatan. Two rows of matachines begin the first son to greet the cross—to my three-year-old eyes a giant cross covered with flowers: san dieguito, jasmines, gardenias, roses, and greenery, recedad, ferns of various kinds, and even sprigs of herbs—romero, albahcar, ruda, strong and familiar—all pinned to the cross as big as a house, wrapped in muslin with the white sheet at the crossbar. The scent of greenery, of so many flowers. I hold Papi's hand, afraid of the noise and the costumed "viejo," when suddenly there he is in front of me with his animal face, brandishing a whip—I let out a scream and hold on to Papi who lifts me up, comforts, "Ya, ya, si es Don José, don't you see?" as he points to the viejo walking away to scare others. My arms around his neck, my tears won't subside, sollozando, I sigh and cry, off and on, all night even when we're home. Bueli's angry at Don José, gives me a spoonful of sugar "pa'l susto." That night it's the fire-eating devil from the pastorela who becomes the viejo of the matachines in my nightmares. I wake up screaming. And the next day Bueli does a healing for susto. A healing unlike Doña Cipriana's, but it works just the same. She sweeps pirul branches over my body, rubs an egg cool as it touches my arms, my legs; mumbles prayers as I lie on the kitchen floor. I sleep soundly. Next day, the egg under the bed reveals the animal face of el viejo, and I am healed.

⤜ Fever ⤛

When we got the measles—or maybe chicken pox—sarampión, all three of us Tino, Dahlia and I got it at the same time. I'm burning; I know what the comal feels like; the fever and the itching so severe even the starch baths don't help. In Bueli's bed, a dream while I'm awake: the bed full of rattlesnakes like the ones Papi kills when they come to our backyard; he hangs them high on the mesquite for rain, snakes that want to wrap around my body, grab my feet, tongues in and out flicking toward me, wanting to bite. I cry soundlessly, and terrified climb the iron headboard seeking to escape until Mami or Bueli comes in, holds me, shows me there are no snakes; it's just the cotton quilt Bueli made last summer from leftover scraps from all of Mami's sewing. "See, here's the piece from your dress for school, and here's a piece from your birthday dress, and here's one from Dahlia's dress, and here's Tino's shirt just like your Papi's," No snakes, here, just the quilt of many colors, bits of fabric that look just like the snake skins Papi dries and keeps. But I don't believe my eyes have lied, so I want the plain muslin sheets, instead; I don't want the quilt anywhere near the bed.

◝ Fridays ◜

On Fridays Papi gets paid at the smelter. So we wait for him to come home, to go to the store owned by "El Brodita" (from little brother) who used to work with Papi and lends money, and lets you sign a paper and take groceries home when there's a strike. It's Friday but we can't eat meat, even though it's pay day and Mami has bought picadillo at El Brodita's. Instead we eat enchiladas with white cheese, and beans, or maybe fish, canned spinach and mashed potatoes. Each one of us gets to buy a candy bar: I pick the red and silver Cracker Jack box with a surprise toy; or maybe a chocolaty Slo Poke that lasts longer. At thirteen, though, such treats no longer attract. One special Friday I ask permission to go with Estér and her family to Nuevo Laredo. We go to México Típico, her Dad drinks beer, her mother Azalia's madrina argues with him. Her brothers laugh and tease us. Estér and I order sidra. I ask for enchiladas because it's Friday; I can't eat meat. They laugh. I don't believe them, it's not a sin in Mexico to eat meat on Fridays. But I ask Papi and he says it's true; it's not a sin. So the next time, I order milanesa con papas, and at age thirteen I begin to question church rules, so arbitrary and unfair. And I ask if covering your hair holds true on both sides, yes, in fact, in Mexico you can't just plop a kleenex on top and secure it with a hairpin—the usher at the church in Monterrey wouldn't let me in until my cousin explained that I was from the United States. Estér's Dad also likes bull-fights, and Estér wants me to go, so I beg and beg permission until Papi relents and I am allowed to go, "But I don't think you'll like them," Mami says. But I do. Love the fanfare, the music, the colors, the people—the serious grey-hatted autoridades, the drunk gringos—and all the ritual. But each time, when it's time to kill the bull, I don't want to look and I feel sick. I never go again.

⌁ Nun's Habit ⌁

Just took communion. Back in my pew between Dahlia and Esperanza on the girls' side of San Luis Rey Church, I pray, eyes closed, feel warm and a little faint. My face bowed, I open my eyes to see a nun's habit—heavy brown fabric, layers and layers of cloth. I feel the starched white collar cut into my neck. I look at my hands, a band of gold on my left ring finger instead of the blue topaz Tía Luz gave me. I feel faint again, a ringing in my ears so loud I think everyone must hear it. I close my eyes and pray, please God, let me be me again. When I open my eyes again, everyone is standing and I am sitting, Doña Julia is on her way to punish. It smarts where she pinches my skinny arm, and I jump to my feet, kneel for the blessing. I don't dare tell anyone what has happened. When I bring up the memory like a treasured secret jewel, I feel sadness and peace at the same time. I don't tell, not Estér, not Anamaría, not Bueli, not Mami, I just hide the memory. When it escapes, sometimes in church, or when I'm walking back from school, I wonder what it would be like to be Sister Consuelo, living without children, not married, praying all the time. Boring, that's what I think. Not what I'd like, and I never really contemplate joining the convent. Besides, by the time I graduate and can think about it, my questions about the church seem endless and unanswerable, and the memory of that hot, heavy, brown habit on my thin frame is but a forgotten dream. Some friends did want to hide in a convent, marry Jesus. Like my friend, now my comadre, Ana, whose parents sent her to Mexico City with relatives when she announced her intentions right after graduation. It worked, too. Ana came back changed, went to college, and forgot about joining the convent. None of Mami's flowers—Azucena, Dahlia, Esperanza, Margarita, Azalia, Teresita, Rosa or Xóchitl—were so inclined. And neither Rolando nor David ever gave the priesthood a thought. At one time Tino could've been swayed into the priesthood. They tried, Brother Joseph, Father Jones, through Boy

Scout camp, through altar boy solidarity, through jobs offered during the summer—jobs that paid wages that Papi paid for. How angry he was when he found out. Sometimes I'm sure Papi wonders what would've happened if Tino had gone to the seminary in high school. Would he have graduated, not gone to war, not been killed? Papi's guilt must've been tremendous. Must be why he blamed me. I, the oldest, the one who spoke English, why didn't I talk to my brother? He usually listened to me. I could've told him not to enlist, to wait till he finished high school, at least. Maybe then something else would've happened. Then Tino comes to say good-bye, I leave my desk in the back office where I work eight-to-five, come up front, and I don't know what to say. "Write," I mumble as I hug him good-bye. Papi, doesn't understand, I'm not to blame. Neither is he, nor Mami. He wants to blame someone. Everyone. And when the purple heart and other medals come with Tino's things, he has them framed, hangs them next to the faded photo of an Army uniformed seventeen-year-old, dreamy eyed, thin-lipped brown face, wearing pride like a badge.

The Beach

We've gone to visit Papi's Tío Pancho in Corpus. The house so big I get lost going from the living room to the kitchen. He is a serious Papagrande, doesn't laugh, my granduncle. We leave. Driving on Shoreline Drive I see the beach. It's winter and the sky is grey; the sand, the water, everything fades into concrete grey. I cry and scream and make Papi stop so I can see the water. He takes my four-year-old hand; wearing a pastel blue coat and hat I sink, walking, running on the sand, gain solid footing as I approach the water's edge. The sound of the wind and the roar of the gulf waves, the spray terrifies and thrills me. "Ya vámonos," I say. And Papi carries me back to the green Ford where Mami and Bueli wait. Mami scolds Papi for spoiling me, granting my every whim, giving in to my crying. I am asleep by the time we arrive at Chelito's where we have fried fish and rice for dinner. He carries me in. I hear the roar of the ocean as they talk and cook. Tomorrow we'll have menudo for breakfast, I hear Chelito declare, and I can smell it cooking.

Cowboy Boots

I don't like cowboy boots. I don't wear cowboy boots, and in fact when I see a man, especially an Anglo, wearing cowboy boots, I cringe, react like I do when someone scratches the chalkboard with their nails. Sanjuana, my childhood friend, was raped by Tom, who chewed tobacco and wore cowboy boots. He and his wife owned a store on Saunders. He was over six feet tall, had a beer belly, and spoke very little Spanish. She was a white Mexican, short, with glasses that hung around her neck with a chain. She went to San Luis Rey Church, even had a posada at their house behind the store one Christmas. But I feared Tom, although he gave us candy if we brought in straight A's on our report card. Sanjuana never said anything, but I knew. I knew even before Helen confirmed it.

Sanjuana quit school when we were all supposed to go on to seventh grade at the junior high; her parents wanted her to stay home and take care of the younger ones, help her mother wash and iron and cook and clean. She did. But then her father got sick, was fired from the smelter and there was no money, not even for food, and they owed Tom for months of food. Sanjuana went to work for Tom. She swept the floor, cleaned the shelves, sliced and weighed cold cuts, made the signs: fire-engine red paint on white butcher paper that advertised "manteca 3#/$1" while we were painting posters for our football games, "Go, Lions, Go." I don't know how I knew since I didn't even know about such things. Mami never talked to me about sex. Although she had curiously enough left a book that explained things on top of the chiffonier—but it was written in a technical medical vocabulary—and in Spanish—and when I read it a escondidas fearing that she'd find out, I never did understand what exactly was happening. But perhaps it was Mami's word of caution after my cousin Lily's experience with a dirty old man, the janitor at her school who was lifting little girls dresses and doing bad things to them, that alerted me. All I know is I knew. And Sanjuana knew I knew. But she never said a word. One time we talked about Chelo who'd eloped, and she just looked away, embarrassed. When she was almost six months pregnant everyone found out. But no one did anything, except Tom's wife, who fired Sanjuana, calling her puta and slut. I was pretending to watch "I Love Lucy" when I overheard Mine telling Mami what had happened. I wanted to go kill him. I asked Helen; she confirmed it, Sanjuana had told her from the very beginning, how he lured her with gifts, promises, then threatened her. Sanjuana. The next day, after school, I went to her house. Her Mother greeted me saying Sanjuana was gone. She was at her aunt's in Nuevo Laredo. My friend was going to have a baby and we couldn't even talk. Her father was gone, he'd signed on to work up north or else he would've killed the gringo, Helen said. A few days later, Mami sent me to the store to get something for dinner because we were making a colcha and had not had time to cook. Tom was perched on his usual stool at the cash register. I was so upset I couldn't look at him. Instead, I just looked down as I signed Mami's name for the pound of baloney and the loaf of bread; all I saw were his cowboy boots.

↶ Susirio ↷

After the cowboy program and the news on Channel 8 in Laredo, and before "Gutierritos," the soap opera, we'd watch Betty Boop and Mighty Mouse cartoons on Channel 2 from Nuevo Laredo. Sitting on the floor eating supper and after having prayed the rosary, we watched the black-and-white screen with the cellophane paper tacked to the front to make it look like color. Hoping for a clearer reception, we fiddled with the rabbit ears like the ones Chole had bought on sale for when she bought her TV. She's either an optimist or a fool, Papi declared. For the news, I'd translate simultaneously for Papi and Mami, also for some shows, like Lawrence Welk, for Bueli. Toño, Sanjuana, Eleazar, Raúl, Nana, Chata, and other neighbor kids arrived around four o'clock to watch the cowboy program. Some stayed to watch the cartoons and some stayed and stayed until ten or eleven when Mami turned off the set and sent them home. Sometimes she and I stayed up till midnight or later; she and Bueli sewing, ironing, crocheting, and I reading, doing homework, or also doing embroidery or other needlework. We would talk, she and Bueli talking of life before, of tomorrow, of people I didn't know, dead before I was born. But I heard the stories and their retelling of them, feeling grown-up staying up so late. After Bueli was gone, we'd stay up as before. Then we'd also talk about Bueli and her stories, remembering her favorite TV programs, her remedios. In high school, Tino and I stayed up to watch "The Avengers" or even Jack Parr; Mami'd stay up too, hardly talking, just thinking, humming a lullaby, rocking the baby to sleep.

⤳ Abijada ⤝

Mami is the madrina, so she and her ahijada, Frances, pose for the first communion photo. Mami made the dress and the veil, worked hard crocheting baby booties and sweaters to save the money to pay for the candle, the rosary, the missal for Frances. Frances. The only one of Comadre María's to have an Anglo name. The nuns in the hospital in Wisconsin understood, "Francisca," and called her "Mary Frances." When their family moved to California, settling in Oakland, Mami almost convinced Papi that we should move too. You can get a job where your arthritis won't flare up so much; the children can go to college for free, she argued to no avail. Papi would not move so far from family. When the Treviños came back to visit a year later, Papi regretted not moving—they were doing so well, even if it was mostly field work, and they were still living with Comadre María's sister. But it was too late, Mami was pregnant again. School had already started. Bueli had died. No, it was better to stay here, "Mas vale malo por conocido, que bueno por conocer." Who knows, what appears good is sometimes worse than what we know is bad.

⤳ Pancho ⤝

Doña Julia raised Pancho, her entenado, as her youngest, for Ramiro was already ten when she took in two-year-old Pancho, when his mother died of pneumonia in the migrant camp in Idaho. She had wanted to take all the children, but saw the impossible strain it would be, and agreed to take only Pancho; Tía Nicha almost took one of the little girls, but Tío Güero forbid her to even consider such a burden. Other families took the other three children. The gringo father sad to have to split up his children, but relieved to know that they would be taken care of by the families who came up each year from South Texas. When Pancho married, the priest called out, "Do you Dwayne, take Maricela . . ." and a

121

murmur ran through San Luis Rey Church, no one had ever known Pancho as Dwayne. But there were his brother and sisters come for the wedding raised all over South Texas, Alice, Kingsville, the Valley, calling him Dwayne. Doña Julia cried, as much as when her other children were married; at the reception she greeted everyone, table by table, making sure they were alright. And when the mariachis arrived, Pancho let out with the yell he was famous for. He was happy. Pancho and Maricela moved in with her at first, but when the first baby, Francisco Dwayne, was born, they built a two-room house in the backyard. Leaving little room for Doña Julia's herbs and plants. But, Pancho didn't want to leave Doña Julia alone. And she didn't want him too far. Until the day she died, before he went off to work and after she'd come home from Mass, Pancho and Doña Julia drank their morning coffee sitting at the oilcloth-covered table, discussing last night's dreams, making plans for the day. On her way back from early morning Mass, she was run over by an Air Force pilot, a young lieutenant from Ohio, speeding to the base on Saunders. He didn't even understand what her last words were, all he could recall was that she said something something, Pancho. Pancho mourned for months, named his first girlchild Julia.

⤳ Healings ⤶

We travel by train to Monterrey first. Then with Tía Luz by bus to Matehuala, and on to the tiny hamlet up in the mountains, finally on donkeys to reach the healer's house. But it isn't only a house; there's a settlement—several huts where her helpers and those who require extended treatments stay. Papi has come to look for healing for his arthritis, for his hands are already twisting into the deformed ravished hands of his old age; his foot hurts so much he can barely walk some days. When he holds a hammer it slips out of his hand, the pain shooting into the joints. At the elementary school where he's learning English, filling page after page with conjugated verbs in his florid writing, he writhes with the pain of holding the pencil. So we have come seeking succor from the healer who has performed miracles. Tía Luz tells of miraculous cures, even cancers. On the wall of the waiting room, letters and paintings, exvotos, telling of her powers, her successes. They come from all over Mexico and the United States, even some from Europe. I read but I am not impressed, not convinced, sharing Mami's skepticism. Then one of the helpers comes for Papi. I'm not allowed in where Mami and Tía Luz will wait, Papi goes into an inner chamber, a curtain separates the two inner rooms. I walk outside, sit under the shade of a tall tree I don't recognize; the cool mountain air refreshes although the sun shines hot in the middle of the afternoon. Red ants file by, scurrying to and fro carrying seeds three times their size. I think of Buelito, ants climbing up his arm, on his bare feet, no ant ever bit him. A young girl my age sits on a chair while her mother picks her head for lice. There's something wrong; the girl's look is empty. She doesn't see me although she looks straight at me. I shudder in the warm sun. Later I will hear the mother tell her story: it's puberty that's causing her Manuelita's illness. They've come from Houston, been here two months, must stay through the winter. The illness came with her menstrual periods. She has a weak head. The mother cries. Mami comforts. Somehow I know there's more that I don't understand. Later I hear Tía Luz tell Mami that the girl Manuelita was raped. But now I walk away, sit under a pine tree. I think of Papi's illness. How he claims the pains began that day in spring when he jumped into the cold Sabinal River water. I think of the remedies he's already tried. How he rubs the joints every night with alcohol, marihuana weed floating in the bottle, and the pains persist. How he had all his teeth extracted believing that would help. It didn't. The healers, the doctors, the shots of cortisone, the ten dollar pills. This won't help either, but he must try. Give it a chance. The healer doesn't charge, but if you want you can give the helpers a donation. There are no buses going back to Matehuala by the time we get back to the village, so we spend the night at a house where we eat corn tortillas and beans with a cheese guisado by the light of the kerosene lamp. I sleep on the floor by the door. Lying there, I see a shooting star: my wish, Papi, get well. I go out to pee behind the little house, I look up at the sky, pick out the constellations—Orion, the Dippers. The Milky Way spans the firmament. Alone, in the moonless night I feel the tears well up and let them come.

↜ *Piojos* ↝

With joyous anticipation I arrive home to find Mamagrande and Tía Lydia visiting from Monterrey. I can't wait to tell Mami the news, so right after kissing the visitors hello, I blurt it out—tengo piojos. I explain that at recess, the nurse who had come from the main office had lined us up for inspection and along with checking our eyes and our ears she had taken a popsickle stick and parted our hair, checking for lice. Just like Sanjuana and Chelito and Peewee, and most of my friends, I too wanted to be sent to the office to get the yellow slip that confirmed we had lice. And when the nurse nodded and pointed to the office, I felt I belonged. Just the same way that I would sometimes misspell a word during spelling bees so that I could go sit with my friends and not have to stay up and be teased later and called teacher's pet. With my announcement, I handed Mami the precious yellow slip with instructions for taking care of the problem, but the instructions were in English. So I translated, down to the gory details of what would happen if I didn't get this problem solved. Poor Mami, here she was trying to impress her mother-in-law and I come and ruin it. Mamagrande was scandalized, but had solutions. She told Mami what kind of soap to buy and proceeded to "espulgar" right then and there. I soon realize the big event was no fun. I had to sit with my head on Mamagrande's lap that smelled of Monterrey, and she would pull and tug at my hair whenever she spotted a liendre or

124

a louse crawling on my scalp. The whole weekend was spent taking care of my problem. By Monday, we all compared notes on what torture having piojos meant—the stinking shampoo, the rough soaps, the pink plastic comb with teeth so fine only the tiniest of lice could get away. Only Olegario teased and bragged that he liked having the critters running on his scalp, and how his hair was so black they could hide really well; but in a few days, he came back with his parents' solution to the problem, a shaved head. From then on he became Pelón, a name he kept through junior high and high school when he fought the dress code so he could wear his hair long. Next time the critters found a home in my hair, I didn't brag nor did I come home with the sense of anticipation I did that first time. I knew better. Sometimes, though, I'd pretend to feel the crawling, itching signs of lice so I could lay my head on Mami or Bueli's lap and feel their gentle fingers caress my hair lovingly and find nothing.

⤙ Memo ⤚

Memo came back from the State Special Education School meaner than ever. Don Guillermo, not wanting to submit him to the cruelty of the other kids, had kept him home from school, for they never knew when he would fall to the ground, twisting, writhing, his mouth foaming, making the guttural sounds of a rabid dog. It was his cross to bear, to have his oldest son, the one to carry his name, so ill and a veritable idiot. And yet he loved his son, and to protect him, only his family and neighbors knew about him. Until at the end of one summer season, one of the pickers, not happy with the way Don Guillermo, the trucker and contractor, handled things for us workers, in anger, reported him to the state, or so the story went. That fall, they came and took Memo away to school. Doña Sofía was glad, for she was tired of having to tend to Memo's every need, as if he were an infant; she felt she neglected the younger children. But at the same time she felt it was her duty to tend to her sick son, so at first she had been opposed to his going away from the family. Who would take care of him better than his mother? But when they told her he would learn to read and write, to feed and dress himself, she relented. Also, they said, she had no choice; Memo had to go to school. It hurt her to see him get in the car with the woman from the state. And she'd cry at night thinking about him at the state school in Corpus, so far away, but then she thought of how freer she was and how he was learning to take care of himself, and she was glad. But when he came back that summer, he had changed, and she wasn't so sure it had been such a good idea. While we picked cotton that year, he remained tied to the truck lest he escape and cause problems with the "mañas" he had learned while he was away. But he also could now feed himself and cuss in English, not just in Spanish—his words suddenly intelligible. I knew bad words were not to be repeated aloud, especially not in front of the adults or the teachers. I had found out that Bueli cussed every time she scolded us or was upset and uttered what sounded like "Cheesus" when I had said the same thing, upset at messing up in a jump-rope game, in front of Mrs. Treviño, who then lectured me about what young ladies should and should not say. Although her comadre Concha sprinkled all conversations with "chingados" and "cabrones"—Santa Cachucha, her favorite expression—Mami forbade us using such language. But Memo would rant and rave and shout these and worse to the four winds while tied to the truck. That fall, Memo didn't go back to the state school. When they came for him he was sick in the hospital. He died that winter, back home; after one of his fits he never regained consciousness, just stopped breathing. Some said it was a miracle he had lived so long. But Doña Sofía thought he would've lived a lot longer if he had never left and she had cared for him with her mother's love.

126

~ René ~

The last summer I spend in Monterrey, Mamagrande and Tía Luz send me to the Instituto de Belleza Nuevo León to learn all about being a beautician. Tía Luz pays the tuition so Cousin Lilia and I gain a skill. We board the early morning San Juan route bus into Monterrey, standing out on the Cadereyta Highway until the avocado-green bus screeches to a halt and we join the passengers on their way to work or school. Lilia's in love with a certain driver, César, so we sometimes wait for his shift. She'll eventually marry, not the driver but the cute and younger ticket collector who works the same shifts as César. And I have a "pretendiente" whose beautiful words and light green eyes make me dream I'm the character in *Espaldas Mojadas*, the pocha who marries the Mexican wetback leaving her border and U.S. existence to become a Mexican with David Silva. We talk as novios do, how when he graduates from medical school, after doing his social service obligation, we'll marry, buy a two-story house, go to Europe for our honeymoon, fill the house with babies. But when I realize René's serious and asks when my parents are going to be in town so he can talk to Papi about our plans, I freak out. I am frightened to imagine myself living the life my married cousins live; I imagine myself married, with babies like Mami, and with a jolt realize I don't want that. Seemingly without reason, René and I fight all the time, then make up. It's normal he says. I become jealous, he retaliates; ugly words and tears and before I know it I'm confiding in Gloria that René and I are finished. Gloria, the friend of my heart. She lives with her grandmother; her mother, father, siblings, live in Dallas, come once a year at Christmas; she stays with her grandmother. We share secrets, gossip, love to do each other's hair. She gives me her picture. We walk, linked arm in arm, to the mercado, lure shoeshine boys with promises of free haircuts, and five pesos. Some brave ones, perhaps the ones who need the money the most agree, walk back with us and sit silently watching in the mirrored wall as

their heads change shape before their very eyes. The teachers walk by and approve or disapprove, a word of caution, "cuidado con ésta parte, es de peligro," or praise, "Sí, así está muy bien." Every morning we study theory, memorizing scientific names, theories of chemical reactions for permanents and dyes, or listen to boring lectures on the history of beauty treatments, of beauty care. Every Friday, exams. I pass all but one with flying colors, except for the ortografía of my written answers where my nonschool learned Spanish is found lacking. I take the one exam I flunk the day René and I break up. But in the annual contest, I win first prize, the judges praising my originality, control of the medium, practicality— Gloria beams under the elaborate beehive, my creation, as she poses for our newspaper photograph. My prize; two liters each of shampoo, conditioner, and lacquer—the "sprai" we use to hold the hair as if in concrete. They last and last. My senior year at Martin High several friends ask what shampoo I use to get such shine, what spray to get such hold. I brag and at seventeen, begin my unofficial job as hairdresser for friends and family. I comb Estér's hair for the George Washington's birthday parade. Fellow classmates in the group picture of our high school newspaper staff sport bouffants. My page boy is sprayed in place and feels like a helmet. I cut Sylvia and Diana's hair the day we play hookey, just to know what it's like, before we graduate. I perm Tía Nicha's hair, neighbors come for hairdos for Saturday night dances. But I am afraid, for I know I don't have a license to do what I do. So, I don't charge, but clients pay anyway; fifty cents here, and fifty cents there. I have spending money. When I retire seventeen years later, I put away my special scissors, give away the permanent curlers, my special gloves. The callous on my scissor finger hard and rough reminds me of Gloria, and those summer afternoons recruiting shoeshine boys and dreaming of a different life, a life married to René, a beauty shop all my own, a two-story house in front of a neighborhood plaza, a life as a Mexican.

⤳ Martin High ⤲

Martin High School cafeteria. December. I've stayed with the school paper staff to work and then attend the Pan American Student Forum's annual posada. In the cafeteria before the party, we kid with the football players and dish out tamales from the pot that Rachel Muñoz's mom has prepared for the posada; the pile of soft warm corn husks grows as we eat dozens and dozens. I bite into the warm corn dough stuffed with pork and nuts and raisins and just the right amount of red chile to give it taste. One after another. Gulp each bite down with a swig of Coke. Laugh at Armando and Nacho's antics. Patsy and Homero sitting quietly to the side talking. We're kidding, relajando, eating, laughing. We go get more tamales, and we all freeze as the photojournalist-to-be snaps the picture: my pink headband holds back a sixties flip, matches the pink dress I've made for the posada, appears white, as white as the hand-knit sweater,

Mami's Christmas gift from the year before. A rare photo where I smile unconsciously showing teeth, the broken tooth—the reason I never smile for photos—unnoticeable. The joy, the happiness of youth, carefree and alone away from adults, shines in our faces. Armando won't come back from Vietnam; Nacho won't become the astronaut he dreams of being; Patsy will marry Homero, have six boys before she's even thirty. My friends and others—Estella, Octaviano, Carolina, Julia, Sandra, Gustavo, Sergio, Raúl, Clemente, Genaro, Julian, Steve, Delia, Aurora, Janice, María, Lupita, Tony, Gilberto—four hundred fifty-five in the class of '65 at Martin High School. We'll battle all kinds of obstacles; some will go to college, become teachers—what else was there for us? Go into business, fall into the routine of lives marrying, moving, parenting, living, or maybe not; and give up and get into trouble; drugs, alcohol, despair. Our kids now dropping out, or in college, running off, marrying, parenting, getting into trouble, living. All of us, the studious and the lazy; the gay ones and the straight ones; and the privileged and the disenfranchised; the daring ones and the cautious; the gregarious and the shy ones; the respectful ones and the iconoclasts; the law breakers and the honest citizens; the violent abusers and the gentle, caring ones; become lawyers, drug dealers, architects, doctors, teachers, wheelers and dealers, employers, unemployed, employees, managers, secretaries, receptionists, linemen and women, mail carriers, office clerks, housewives, telephone operators, ranchers, vaqueros, cooks, principals, counselors, professors, social workers, army lifers, nurses, bankers, morticians, police officers. Some of us die in 'Nam, others in childbirth; some die in car accidents, others OD; some go to prison, others go to Europe; some retire at forty-five and go back to school. Suicide, AIDS. We are victims, perpetrators, embezzlers, philanthropists, humanitarians, politicians, healers, hunters, watercolorists, musicians. And the clowns in '65 still clown around at the class reunion in 1990. And some of us never leave, and some of us never come back. Some of us keep coming back. Some of us love, and some of us hate, some of us both love and hate our borderlands. Some of us remember, some of us forget.